SHADOW JUSTICE

Recent Titles in
Contributions in Political Science
Series Editor: Bernard K. Johnpoll

The Liberal Future in America: Essays in Renewal
Philip Abbott and Michael B. Levy, editors

A Change of Course: The West German Social Democrats and NATO,
1957–1961
Stephen J. Artner

Power and Policy in Transition: Essays Presented on the Tenth An-
niversary of the National Committee on American Foreign Policy in
Honor of Its Founder, Hans J. Morgenthau
Vojtech Mastny, editor

Ideology and Soviet Industrialization
Timothy W. Luke

Administrative Rulemaking: Politics and Processes
William F. West

Recovering from Catastrophes: Federal Disaster Relief Policy and
Politics
Peter J. May

Judges, Bureaucrats, and the Question of Independence: A Study of
the Social Security Administration Hearing Process
Donna Price Cofer

Party Identification, Political Behavior, and the American Electorate
Sheldon Kamieniecki

Without Justice for All: The Constitutional Rights of Aliens
Elizabeth Hull

Neighborhood Organizations: Seeds of a New Urban Life
Michael R. Williams

The State Politics of Judicial and Congressional Reform: Legitimiz-
ing Criminal Justice Policies
Thomas Carlyle Dalton

With Dignity: The Search for Medicare and Medicaid
Sheri I. David

American Prince, American Pauper: The Contemporary Vice-Presi-
dency in Perspective
Marie D. Natoli

SHADOW JUSTICE

The Ideology and Institutionalization of Alternatives to Court

CHRISTINE B. HARRINGTON

Contributions in Political Science, Number 133

GREENWOOD PRESS
Westport, Connecticut · London, England

Library of Congress Cataloging in Publication Data

Harrington, Christine B.
  Shadow justice.

  (Contributions in political science, ISSN 0147-1066 ;
no. 133)
  Bibliography: p.
  Includes index.
  1. Neighborhood justice centers—United States.
2. Dispute resolution (Law)—United States.   3. Courts—
United States.   I. Title.   II. Series.
  KF9084.H37   1985   347.73   84-27923
  ISBN 0-313-24332-8 (lib. bdg.) 347.307

Library of Congress Catalog Card Number: 84-27923
ISBN: 0-313-24332-8
ISSN: 0147-1066

First published in 1985

Greenwood Press
A division of Congressional Information Service, Inc.
88 Post Road West
Westport, Connecticut 06881

Printed in the United States of America

10 9 8 7 6 5 4 3 2 1

Contents

Figure and Tables

Acknowledgments

In the process of digging in the archives at the Association of the Bar of the City of New York Library, observing dispute processing in Kansas City, and reading about theories of the state, I met many people, who made the different levels of informal justice and its complexities apparent. These discoveries were the best things about working on this book.

I am particularly grateful to my teachers who continually provided me with important criticism and challenging questions: Joel Grossman, Murray Edelman, David Trubek, Malcolm Feeley, and Robert Gordon. Their comments on earlier drafts and our lively discussions helped unravel the rhetoric of judicial reform and give political meaning to the symbols of informalism.

John Brigham identified early on the shift in judicial reform toward market strategies, and with Don Brown he edited *Policy Implementation: Penalties or Incentives?* (1980), Sage Publication, which includes parts of Chapter 4. He has been a real partner and a great source of encouragement and insight. Rick Abel created an exciting environment for this work; he brought scholars together in his two edited volumes, *The Politics of Informal Justice* (1982), Academic Press, in which portions of

Chapter 2 appear. Parts of Chapter 5 appeared in 16 *Law and Policy* (1984).

I also want to thank other colleagues who commented on parts of the manuscript, especially Richard Hofrichter, Austin Sarat, and Susan Silbey. Two very special friends, Randy Garber and Margaret Hedstrom, always claimed they had an interest in the politics of informal justice. Thanks.

Of course without the access to court records, opportunities to observe mediation hearings and so on, parts of this book would not have been possible. I first want to thank the staff of the Kansas City Neighborhood Justice Center, in particular Terry Evans and Michael Thompson, and the evaluators, David Sheppard and Barbara Kuszmaul. They provided me with a place to work, information about their services, and the freedom to observe the operations of their program. I also must thank the court administrator, the prosecutors and judges of the Municipal Court, and the Kansas City Police Department for their candid comments about the lower court work process, implementing diversion-like reforms and handling everyday disturbances. I am particularly grateful to Jack Schrimsher, the Head Prosecutor, for allowing me to interview his staff, and Ben Midgley from the Computer Division of the Kansas City Police Department for the valuable time he put into responding to the requests of a social scientist. Finally, I thank Howard Eisberg and his law firm for introducing me to the Kansas City legal culture and providing me with a place to stay.

The research was supported in part by the Institute for Research on Poverty at the University of Wisconsin, the American Judicature Society, and the Rutgers University Research Council.

SHADOW JUSTICE

Introduction

Since the 1970s we have been witnessing a reform campaign directed at the administration of justice. Known as delegalization, the reforms emphasize the need to shift our resources and approach away from formal, adversary proceedings and toward informalism and mediation. As a result of reforms that have come about over the last decade there are now "alternative dispute resolution" programs throughout the United States at the local, state, and federal levels. The types of disputes that have come under this delegalization movement range from individuals' interpersonal disputes to conflicts between nations. The scope of this reform is broad and the organization of the movement is fragmented. Both characteristics, some believe, make it difficult to talk about alternative dispute resolution as a movement or field. This book, however, focuses on an area of alternative dispute resolution that reflects the dominant ideology and institutionalization of informalism—the neighborhood justice center.

The social conflicts brought to the neighborhood justice center are the minor criminal and civil complaints told to police, prosecutors, and lower court judges. The conflicts that surface, or become visible, as minor disputes are so pervasive in everyday life that they may seem invisible. Yet, the tasks associated with regulating everyday social conflict raise issues of social justice and present challenges to the maintenance of social order. For those facing the latter challenges, these tasks include identifying minor conflicts so they can be defused before they escalate and channeling disputes that have emerged from the social fabric to the appropriate remedy system. For example, police frequently respond to neighborhood complaints and domestic disturbances by getting the parties to "keep the peace" without arrest. This activity has been called "order maintenance" by James Q. Wilson (1968) and it differs from "law enforcement" in his scheme because it does not involve arrest for such things as disorderly conduct or simple assault. The state often performs these tasks without involving the law directly. Indeed, judges, prosecutors, and other actors in the judicial system perform the tasks of order maintenance without directly employing legal sanctions.

This book examines state policy on informal dispute processing in the twentieth century. The reforms associated with informalism and the ideology itself are found to be closer to an order maintenance style of exercising state authority than to matters of social justice. The study of alternative dispute resolution, therefore, links the practice of order maintenance and delegalization reforms. The links are established here through an analysis of the ideology of informalism (Part I), the institutional organization of legal resources (Part II), and a case study of a neighborhood justice center (Part III).

In Chapter 1, judicial reform ideology is treated as a social practice, not a set of idealized reform goals. From a materialist concept of ideology we examine the institutional boundaries of this reform. The ideology of informalism is structured by its relationship to delegalization movements and order maintenance concerns. Although the style and language of mediation are different, mediation is less distinct from traditional legal forms than the reformers recognize. Ostensibly replacing formalism as an ideology, informalism retains a legalistic core that ties it to conventional practice. This does not mean that delegalization reform movements have simply duplicated existing dispute-processing forums. The movement does reflect a transformation in the way disputes are thought of and handled. The issues to be explored in the first part of this study are the nature and significances of this transformation.

In Chapter 2, dispute-processing reform is seen in the broader social and political contexts in which it develops: the rise of judicial management in the Progressive period and the reconstruction of court unification in the 1970s. In the Progressive period, the principles of scientific management were introduced in informal dispute-processing reform. The reform movement attempted to replace the Justice of the Peace Courts with informal branches of the Municipal Court, such as the Small Claims Court and the Domestic Relations Court. Specialized informal tribunals centralized judicial management over minor social conflicts. In the 1970s, efforts to reconstruct judicial management shifted toward a decentralized management model. The neighborhood justice movement developed in the context of decentralized judicial supervision over minor disputes. Along with Chapter 3, these considerations draw attention to the institutional organization of legal resources in Part II.

The politics of defining legal resources and determining how they will be distributed in alternative dispute resolution policy is the focus of Chapter 3. The policymaking process by which national goals on minor dispute processing were developed is examined. The particular reformers and the proposals generated by their interests in neighborhood justice centers are identified as are the ways that such seemingly diverse reform groups were able to develop a common program under the Dispute Resolution Act (1980). Experiments in alternative dispute resolution, ranging from mediating racial disputes to establishing institutional grievance processes, provide a context for understanding the politics of national policy on dispute resolution.

Chapters 4 and 5 turn to a case study of a neighborhood justice center established in 1978 as a pilot program by the U.S. Department of Justice. These two chapters, which make up Part III, apply propositions about informalist ideology, developed in Part I and Part II, to a case study of dispute-pro-

cessing reform. Specifically, Chapter 4 shows the institutionalization of voluntarism in the Neighborhood Justice Center
referral network. This results from the Neighborhood Justice
Center's dependence on the judicial system for its cases. The
claim that these forums expand access to justice is based largely
on the assertion that neighborhood justice centers are different from lower courts.

Unlike small claims court and housing court, these [mediation] programs are not watered-down versions of real courts. Their roots are
not in Anglo-American jurisprudence, but in the African moots, in
socialist comrades courts, in psychotherapy and in labor mediation
(Felstiner and Williams, 1980:1).

In Chapter 5, the issue of expanding access to justice through
increased participation in dispute processing is explored. The
rates of participation and nonparticipation in mediation hearings and court hearings for related party cases are compared.
The Neighborhood Justice Center reproduces patterns of participation in dispute processing found in the lower court and
both share a similar structure of sanctions. The Neighborhood
Justice Center confronts the same problems the lower court
faces in getting both parties in related party disputes to participate in dispute processing. The similarities are only a sur-
prise because the ideology of informalism makes so much of
the differences.

Despite fear that our society is becoming overly litigious, social scientists have suspected for some time now and we are
beginning to document more clearly that the bulk of criminal
and civil dispute processing within the judicial system is not
carried out through formal adjudication processes. This
knowledge challenges the hysteria of those who fear litigiousness, and more importantly, I think, it directs attention to examining the social and political meanings of juridical practices.

This book begins with the understanding that dispute resolution is a political resource. It seeks to further this perspective on law and politics by examining the ideology and institutionalization of order maintenance practices of dispute

processing. The book examines the kinds of disputes that linger on the boundaries of the judicial system, how these are handled, and what social interests are served. The result is a portrayal of "shadow justice" as a form of state power.

Part I

REFORM IDEOLOGY

CHAPTER ONE

Courts and the Ideology of Informalism

Hostile pronouncements on lower courts are far from uncommon. They are the main ingredient in campaigns to improve the administration of justice, the catalyst of judicial reform. Reformers have compiled testimony on the inefficiencies and injustices of lower courts from the elite of the legal profession to the battered woman who files a complaint. Assaults on lower courts are so widespread that we readily accept Roscoe Pound's characterization of them as "popular" dissatisfactions. Attacks on courts are so common that they have become an ordinary part of American political life. The ordinariness of complaints about courts explains, in part, why reformers have been able to mobilize general support for judicial reforms.[1]

Discontent with courts and a desire to reorganize them is not new. Indeed, the contemporary movement against legal formalism parallels the reforms proposed and instituted between 1900 and 1930.[2] These early reforms were based on sociological jurisprudence, an ideology hostile to legal formalism. Roscoe Pound voiced his distaste for the "sporting theory of justice" in his famous critique on the causes of popular dissatisfaction with the administration of justice (Pound, 1906). He argued that legal formalism failed to produce agreements based on shared underlying values and therefore it encouraged the instrumental use of law.

The effect of our exaggerated contentious procedure is not only to ir-
ritate parties, witnesses and jurors in particular cases, but to give to
the whole community a *false notion of the purpose* and end of law. . . .
If the law is a mere game, neither the players who take part in it nor
the public who witness it can be expected to yield to its spirit when
their interests are served by evading it. . . . Thus the courts, instituted to administer justice according to law, are made agents or
abettors of lawlessness (Pound, 1906:406; emphasis added).

This has become a common and recurrent complaint. Seventy
years later Nonet and Selznick agree.

A formalist, rule-bound institution is ill equipped to recognize what
is really at stake in its conflicts with the environment. It is likely to
adapt opportunistically because it lacks criteria for rational reconstruction of outmoded or inappropriate policies. . . . The idea of legality needs to be conceived more generally and to be cured of formalism (Nonet and Selznick, 1978:77, 108).

The principal objection to legal formalism in both periods is
that the substantive ideals invoked on behalf of *legality* in a
liberal democracy (equality, justice, and liberty) conflict with
legalization (the extension of procedural rules governing the
processing of disputes). The extension of legal rights is opposed on the grounds that the formal rationality of law and
courts fails to provide substantive justice. Consequently, the
reform movements have favored *delegalization.*
   However consistently critical of and concerned with formalism these reform movements have been, they have preserved
some of the basic characteristics of the legalistic paradigm.
In neither period has delegalization reform sought to *replace*
the legalistic paradigm (Shklar, 1964) of dispute processing.
On the contrary, the reforms have been designed to complement the existing adjudication processes. Advocates of delegalization justify their proposals as reconciling, harmonizing,
and balancing formal justice and social justice. Instead of fundamentally challenging formalism, the classic tension within
liberal legalism between procedural and substantive rationality is revealed during these reform periods (Abel, 1979).[3]

MAKING REFORM IDEOLOGY PROBLEMATIC

The approach in this book has been shaped by the notion that reform ideology is itself problematic and linked to institutional practices. The politics of delegalization cannot be uncovered by contrasting idealized categories with practice, by using the goals of informalism as the standard for evaluating its practice. "Gap" studies tell us more about the ideals of reform than about the politics of alternative dispute resolution. Nor can we understand the politics of delegalization by simply focusing on the type of disputes that are diverted to informal tribunal. *The reform goal of informalism is itself problematic.* The reform ideology and institutions mediate political tensions and reflect contradictory aspects of the reform movement.

Gaps

Our understanding of this reform has been affected by the inclination to look for gaps when appraising informal dispute-processing institutions. In studies of how *successful* alternative dispute resolution is, we have been preoccupied with evaluating the implementation of and compliance with reform goals. For example, studies of informalism introduced in the Progressive period examine the *rhetoric* of Progressive reformers and contrast it with the *reality* of the institutions they developed. Scholarly accounts attribute the failure of the juvenile court to the optimism of Progressive reform (Ryerson, 1978; Rothman, 1980). Noting the tension within the Progressive platform between humane ideals and the desire for an administratively efficient mechanism for handling juveniles, scholars have emphasized the gap between the reform model and the juvenile courts.

Similarly, studies of Small Claims Court reform conclude that Progressive reformers failed in their missions to create a truly nonadversarial dispute process, because they did not question "the *kind* of process through which small claims—whether those of rich or poor—are being handled, and thus have left intact a cornerstone of the small claims hearing, the adversary process" (Yngvesson and Hennessey, 1975:263). This oversight has correctly been attributed to the "cross-cutting interests" of the legal profession (Ibid.). But once again this approach uses the goals of informalism as the standard for evaluating the success or failure of the reform movement.[4]

The subject of analysis—informalism—becomes the criterion for judging the reform. Informal procedures are idealized as nonadversarial, rehabilitative, and preventative methods for resolving conflict. The reform goal—informalism—is treated as nonproblematic and, invariably, analysis centers on barriers to implementing this goal. This approach leads to predictable and unilluminating evaluations of the politics of reform. That the juvenile courts and Small Claims Court movements did not institutionalize the ideals of informalism does not mean they were simply failed reforms. Clearly both have had significant consequences for lower courts as well as for the people who use them.

Samuel Walker's history of criminal justice administration begins with a similarly idealized conception of the Progressive period (Walker, 1980). Borrowing Herbert Packer's categories, Walker argues that tensions within the Progressive movement were the result of a conflict between an "efficiency-oriented crime-control" model and a "due process orientation." Yet he argues that "both shared a 'system' approach to the administration of criminal justice, and for both sides, the system perspective fostered the nationalization of crime control" (Ibid.:128). This approach escapes the dominant tendency to reduce tensions or contradictions within reform movements to static and often dualistic concepts (adversarial and nonadversarial, formal and informal). Walker is able to explain this reform as part of a *transformation* in the administration of criminal justice—the development of a systems approach. The tensions evidenced in Progressive reforms characterized this transformation rather than representing its "failure."

Another dominant approach to analyzing informal procedures emphasizes the *type* of dispute as the unit of analysis. For example, commentaries on the juvenile court movement are primarily concerned with the relationship between Progressive ideology and adolescent socialization (see Platt, 1969; Fox, 1970; Mannel, 1973; Schultz, 1973; Faust and Brantingham, 1974; Ryerson, 1978; Rothman, 1980). Youth became a new object of social attention during this period, meriting closer scrutiny by the courts and requiring a distinct legal environment. Such studies suggest that the particular kind of conflict (juvenile) is the major determinant of dispute-processing styles. However, the application of informal procedures during this period was hardly limited to the juvenile, nor did Progressive reformers believe that such procedures were suitable for juvenile cases alone. Without diminishing the importance of justifications for adopting informal procedures in juvenile cases, I want to shift the emphasis to the structural constraints of this reform on the ideology and institutionalization of dispute processing for particular types of cases.

The Perspective

A sociological perspective on legal ideology informs this study of the relationship between the ideology and institutions of informalism. This perspective leads to the examination of the content of ideology and its role in securing the conditions for the exercise of power. Roger Cotterrell elaborates on this approach, noting that a sociological perspective looks at legal ideology "from the outside." The objective is to identify "the conditions under which ideologies develop, are sustained and disintegrate because of the sociological and politically practical significance of this knowledge" (Cotterrell, 1983a:70). We are concerned with the structures of reform ideology and their political significance.

In the process of identifying the underlying social relations constituting legal ideology, the instrumental tendency to reduce the ideology of informalism to a mere social control function (e.g., rationalization, legitimation) must be avoided. Those who have worked on the concept of legal ideology more directly point out that "we should abandon any *a priori* views about its [law's] integrative or legitimating functions and treat them as open questions relating to understanding the specific effects or consequences of legal regulation and legal ideology"

(Hunt, 1985:17–18).[5] Roger Cotterrell also warns us to avoid an over-determined model of the functions of legal ideology. He argues that "while Weber is correct in pointing out the partially self-sustaining character of legal domination in certain circumstances, this is not a consequence of the inevitability of rationalization as an unchallengeable necessity removed from influence by human will, but is, to a significant extent, the consequence of ideological effects of law which help to create conditions under which the range of choice of action and the expectations of individuals are normally seriously conceived only within the limits of the conception of society and social relations embodied in legal ideology" (Cotterrell, 1983a:82).

In her research on civil courts Maureen Cain applies a framework that incorporates these cautions. She suggests that civil courts can be seen as doing "conceptive ideological work" as opposed to rationalizing legal domination. Dispute processing in these courts "re-affirm[s] the legal construction of those relationships which are presented to [the court] *by a particular set of users*. On occasion these relationships are new, or for some reason require re-interpretation. Then the work of the civil court is creative, and legal status is given to the emergent relationships, which the users of the court are creating or in which they find themselves. This is conceptive ideological work: using old rules to generate new ways of thinking, of making sense of, and thereby of constituting ideologically new and emergent material forms" (Cain, 1983:131).

The ideology of informalism constitutes a "new and emergent material form," it is not simply the hopes and promises of overly optimistic reformers. It is a social construction.[6] In this chapter the content of reform ideology and the conditions under which it develops are examined. This analysis includes a study of challenges to the legitimacy of lower courts, and a discussion of how such challenges have influenced both the form and content of the alternatives movement.

SOCIAL TRANSFORMATIONS AND JUDICIAL REFORM

The ideology of informalism in the twentieth century is about the scope and nature of *judicial power* and *judicial authority*.[7] Frank Munger identifies two dimensions that characterize judicial reform in this period. One is "defined by the emphasis placed on preserving the autonomy and special expertise of court adjudication—that is, on legalism" (Munger, 1982:54). The second dimension is defined by "the emphasis placed on access to courts, on making them more available for dispute settlement" (Ibid.:55). The authority of legalism and the boundaries of judicial access are also two dimensions of the ideology of informalism. The construction of informal ideology is linked to the reconstruction of judicial power and authority.

The task of orchestrating a system for adjudicating conflict that questions the utility of formalism calls for different principles of legitimacy *and* the reorganization of a legal consensus. Like legal formalism, the legitimacy of delegalization reforms is still grounded in procedure, but, in contrast to formalism, these procedures are characterized as "informal alternatives" (Aaronson et al., 1977; Garth, 1982). This reform, however, is not simply a patchwork effort to reestablish the "legitimacy" of judicial institutions in a democratic society. It is also a reform to increase judicial power. It builds a new basis for both legitimating authority and expanding the power of the *judicial system*.

Rallying around the Crisis

"Court crisis" is the key judicial reform metaphor in twentieth century struggles to expand judicial power and authority. These struggles are waged under the banner of court crisis. The phrase essentially refers to threats to the legitimacy of judicial institutions. For example, to diffuse public criticism of courts as well as complaints by private commercial groups,[8] the Progressives urged that lower courts adopt "business-like" management. New York City Court Judge William Ransom, a

Progressive, commenting on public opinion in general and the
views of business groups in particular, said with disapproval:
"Instead of bringing methods for ascertaining facts and determining controversies, public opinion took the performance of
essentially judicial functions away from the courts" (Ransom,
1917a:145).[9] Eleven years earlier Pound made a similar observation in his famous speech on the causes of popular dissatisfactions with the administration of justice:

Public opinion must affect the administration of justice through the
rules by which justice is administered rather than through the direct
administration. All interference with the uniform and automatic application of these rules, when actual controversies arise, introduces
an anti-legal element which becomes intolerable (Pound, 1906:400).

Once again, judicial reformers today talk of a court crisis and
question the appropriateness of formal adjudication for resolving minor disputes and distributing mass justice. The the-
oretical attacks on formalism (Nonet and Selznick, 1978) and
the programmatic development of alternative dispute
resolution[10] are both part of a larger reform wave that advocates "deinstitutionalization" (see Scull, 1977). The recent development of tribunals for minor disputes between parties in
ongoing relationships (e.g., domestic, neighborhood, con-
sumer-merchant, landlord-tenant, employment) is one expression of the movement for less formal methods of dispute processing.

The alternative dispute resolution movement shares the
perspective of the reformers. Its central thesis is that the adversarial structure and adjudicatory function of courts prohibit effective representation and resolution of related party
disputes. This thesis is derived from a traditional interpretation of judicial decision making. Mediation is also portrayed
as having a distinctive structure and function. It is characterized as being an accommodating and flexible process that allows disputants the opportunity to bargain and make compro-
mises not available to them in the adjudicatory process. The
authority structure of mediation depends on sanctions and incentives within the disputants relationship rather than exter-

nal standards and rules (Fuller, 1971; 1978). Individual circumstances and histories shape the outcome of informal mediation instead of general and neutral principles that constitute the judicial method (Sander, 1977). This structure allows problem solving rather than chooses a winner and a loser. Accordingly, the function of mediation is to focus on future behavior. This type of orientation, it is argued, reduces conflict rather than escalating social tensions and thereby responds to the court crisis (Aaronson et al., 1977).

What are the sources of this so-called anti-legal criticism of the courts? Under what conditions does informalism in the twentieth century transform the scope of judicial power and the basis of institutional authority through a court crisis?

Sources of Anti-Legal Criticism

The growth in the early 1880s of arbitration tribunals independent of the courts notified reformers that business had a strong aversion to courts.[11] Progressives argued that the failure of legislatures to enact provisions creating simplified judicial procedures for handling commercial disputes led to the expansion of private arbitration tribunals. Delay, congestion, and "formality" in procedures were continually cited as the reasons why conservative, law-abiding businessmen were "ready to 'settle for fifty percent' of the amount in dispute rather than be subject to 'a law suit,' even in a court which has been considered peculiarly the 'business man's court' in the metropolis" (Ransom, 1917b:199). Judge Ransom believed that courts were not in tune with business practices. He said in the "past fifty years we have revolutionized our methods of the conduct of private business, and largely also the conduct of public business; our methods are more direct, exact, and to the point; they minimize the possibility of error, eliminate 'lost motion' and cut 'red tape.' Yet to all this improvement in method our judicial procedure has paid substantially no heed" (Ibid.:199).

Reformers viewed the disjuncture between commercial methods and judicial administration as a "crisis" for courts. Lacking adequate procedures for intervening in commercial disputes in a manner acceptable to business interests, the judiciary was handicapped in shaping economic relations during the transition from merchant to corporate capitalism.[12] On another level, lower courts were isolated from everyday life (the mass of small transactions) by what reformers called the "doctrine of contentious procedure" (Harley, 1912b; Hurst, 1953). Reformers believed that the legitimacy of courts suffered as a result of delay in processing claims (court congestion) and that the situation might become intolerable if left unremedied.

Percy Werner, a member of the Missouri Bar, argued that although lawyers had "instinctively turned against this method [arbitration] of disposing of private differences, as being unscientific, as any adjudication by non-experts must be," they should not oppose *all* arbitration (Werner, 1914:278). Private arbitration tribunals might be considered symbols of an antilegal bias, but judges and lawyers dedicated to professionalization could still endorse constitutional amendments and statutory provisions establishing *judicial* arbitration. Many state and local bar associations began to pass resolutions in the early 1900s encouraging "the bar and business men generally to pull together in each locality for the prevention of unnecessary litigation" by providing information about ways to prevent disputes from arising (*JAJS*, 1919b:158). Werner proposed that "voluntary tribunals" be established by the Bar, with lawyers serving as arbitrators (Werner, 1914:279). The Joint Committee of the Chamber of Commerce Committee on Arbitration of the State of New York and the New York State Bar Association Committee on Prevention of Unnecessary Litigation was formed in 1916. "Backed by the brains of the New York bar and the money of the New York merchant," they drafted a proposal for judicial arbitration of commercial disputes (Robbins, 1916:280). Disputes concerning contracts, wills, licenses, and insurance policies were all designated as appropriate for arbitration. Other commercial arbitration boards, such as those promoted by the Chicago Association of Credit Men, were established with either the assistance or approval of the Bar (*JAJS*, 1918a). The Association of the Bar of the City of New York was active in supporting the creation of the Arbitration Society of America in 1922, described by the American Judicature Society as comprised of "men prominent on the bench, at the bar and in the business world . . . unite[d] to promote voluntary adjudication under arbitration statutes" (*JAJS*, 1922a:59). In addition, many states passed arbitration statutes modeled on the commercial arbitration proposals drafted by the American Judicature Society (see Willoughby, 1929:64–75).

These reforms were part of a strategy to "reestablish" the lost jurisdiction and credibility of courts (Potter, 1922). Unable to keep pace with the changing needs of commercial interests, the judicial *method* itself became the target for critics. Judge Ransom observed that "business men go to arbitration to avoid legal *procedure* and not legal principles" (Ransom, 1917b:201). Procedural formality, according to the Progressives, was the primary source of anti-legal criticism by the private sector. Proposals for judicial arbitration were offered by the organized Bar as a means of preserving legal principles while avoiding the problems of legalization.

The crisis of the courts was characterized as judicial inaction. Reformers argued that judicial nonintervention, resulting from the doctrine of contentious procedure, prevented courts from affirming the principles of legality. They believed that courts, by failing to sustain institutional legitimacy on procedural grounds (the essence of formal rationality), faced a crisis of legitimacy. The *form* of judicial intervention, therefore, became the central issue of the delegalization movement.

The organization of a new legal consensus encompassed more than the advocacy of an ideology of judicial intervention through informal methods. It also required the creation of *institutional structures* to implement informal dispute processing. Arbitration, supervised by the legal profession and sanctioned by state institutions and laws, was proposed as the form of intervention to rebuild the legitimacy of a legal consensus and expand jurisdiction over everyday commercial disputes.

Just as the reform criticism of judicial passivity transformed commercial dispute processing, so too did this kind of anti-legal criticism transform the judicial channels of access to justice for minor criminal and civil disputes. Joined by the legal aid societies, Progressives attacking the doctrine of contentious procedure applied their view of judicial inaction to a second set of forces generating a crisis of the courts: the growth of urban immigrant workers and the poor. The problems of public order in the new urban economy were met with proposals for a more active judiciary.

Reformers maintained that there was no justice for the poor in either the inferior courts or the rural Justice of the Peace Courts. The former were depicted as too expensive, dilatory, and remote from the problems of the new urban working class. The latter were condemned as corrupt, arbitrary, and lawless (Smith, 1919a; Scott, 1923; Maguire, 1926). They drew attention to the massive number of "petty," urban conflicts that were ignored by the judiciary. Smith, in particular, pointed to the political consequences of judicial inaction:

Claims of this sort are often contemptuously spoken of as "petty litigation." But it is in this very field that the courts have their greatest political effect. In every urban community these are the cases of the large majority of citizens. As they are treated well or ill, so they form their opinion of American judicial institutions (Smith, 1919a:42).

Pound also pointed to political and social effects of judicial institutions. He called for the "socialization of law" in order to "secure social interests in the modern city" (Pound, 1913:311). By this he meant that laws had to be created by society to "protect men from themselves, to regulate housing, to enforce sanitation, to inspect the supply of milk, to prevent imposition upon ignorant and credulous immigrants" (Ibid.). This was true whether the problems involved wage claims by workers or the "relations of family life, where conditions of crowded urban life and economic pressure threaten the security of the social institutions of marriage and the family" (Ibid.:323). The scope of judicial administrations would be enlarged by the "socialization of law."

The campaigns to "Americanize" the immigrant, rehabilitate the delinquent, the deviant, and the discontent are examples of programs for the socialization of law (Smith, 1919a). One of the first active Americanizing groups, the North American Civil League for Immigrants (1907), focused public attention on the political significance of "petty litigation" and the role of courts in processing such conflict. The league was a private philanthropic organization formed to represent Northeastern conservative economic interests (Hartmann, 1948:38). In 1908 Frances Kellor, a member of the league, was appointed to the New York State Immigration Commission by Governor Charles Evans Hughes and charged with directing research on the relationship of immigrants to criminal and civil law. As a result of its study the commission established the New York State Bureau of Industries and Immigration (1910). Kellor described this bureau as an "immigrants court" (Kellor, 1914:168). Unlike the inferior courts, however, this government agency served as "mediator in bringing together the disputants in cases concerning immigrants" and was "authorized to publish and distribute information which would facilitate assimilation" (Hartmann, 1948:70). Other private organizations, such as the Charity Organization Society of New York City, established joint committees with government agencies to investigate and recommend legislation on dispute resolution and the Americanization of the immigrant (Paddon, 1920).

Remarking on the 1915 reform of the magistrates' courts in New York City, a Philadelphia lawyer described their socializing influence:

Due regard has been had for the psychological value of a proper setting for such courts, in giving the magistrates dignified and sanitary courtrooms or buildings. In this way the value of these magistrates' courts as an Americanizing influence over the foreign elements—of many races and nationalities—in New York City population, is fairly well secured (Shick, 1926:116).

Reformers concerned with legal aid for the poor shared this view. Reginald Heber Smith, reporting to the Conference of Bar Association Delegates in 1924 on the work of the Committee on Small Claims and Conciliation, hailed Small Claims Courts as socialization agents worth more to the cause of Americanization than any amount of talk (Smith, 1924a:14). Similarly, juvenile and family courts were developed to stabilize the family and, through that essential institution, integrate the immigrant into a middle-class American life (see Paddon, 1920; Roberts, 1920; Hartmann, 1948). In addition to being part of the policy for the *socialization* of law, informal dispute processing also was perceived as a socializing force.

To provide access to justice, the barrier of cost had to be overcome. At the same time, the reformers needed a forum that could draw legitimacy from the law but remain flexible enough to absorb minor social conflict in a new urban economy. The Progressives were convinced that the problems they faced in designing an urban judicial system for absorbing such conflict were essentially managerial. Commenting on the virtues of informal procedures, Judge Manuel Levine of the Conciliation Court of Cleveland expressed support for this perspective:

One thing is certain: we cannot even hope to render justice without first having a clear conception as to what justice means. There are many classical definitions, but it took a commercial age to discover that in the main it is merely a problem of correct bookkeeping. We have come to realize in both the criminal as well as the civil work of courts, that justice is the art or science of obtaining human or social balances (Levine, 1915:11).

The justifications for the socialization of law through informal dispute processing were based on two conceptions of access to justice that reinforced the expansion of judicial power through administrative forms, while seeking to legitimate this new form of judicial intervention. One concept of access to justice was explicitly based on an administrative rationale. Reformers maintained that by streamlining both institutions and procedures administrative efficiencies would provide greater access to justice. The familiar phrase "justice delayed is justice denied" and the characterization of justice as "the frictionless movement of a well lubricated machine" reflect an administrative approach to access. The second concept also shares this administrative rationale but to legitimize judicial intervention in a liberal democracy reformers also appealed to participatory ideals. Progressives believed that law would be a more effective socializing agent if citizens participated more directly in informal proceedings.

Both concepts of access to justice are important for analyzing the transformation in minor dispute processing in the Progressive period and in the contemporary delegalization movement. They are attacks on an alleged propensity of Americans
to take minor disputes to court, or "litigiousness." They are also
justifications for accommodating these disputes in other types
of legal institutions. Contrary to what some commentators have
observed, attention to litigiousness is not unique to the current period of reform, indeed the language of litigiousness is
found in the Progressive movement as well.[13] What is often
overlooked is how the rhetoric of litigiousness is part of the
court crisis reform strategy. It preserves the *courts* for certain
types of disputes and creates informal institutions within the
judicial system to handle other types of disputes.

There are, nonetheless, subtle differences between judicial
reform in the Progressive period and the contemporary delegalization movement. Munger distinguishes these periods in
terms of the level of political mobilization surrounding demands for justice:

Unlike the previous periods, the problem [in the recent period] has
been the number of different issues and divergent interests for which
political support was mobilized. The political institutions have been
unable to resolve them all satisfactorily or even to integrate them into
the existing party system to reduce the number of conflicting positions (Munger, 1982:61).

The demands that threatened the courts in the Progressive
period were more effectively organized following the political
and legal mobilization of the poor, women, blacks, environ-
mentalists, consumers, and other interest groups in the 1960s–
1970s.

THE CRISIS OF COURT CAPACITY

The reform ideology in the neighborhood justice movement
of the 1970s to the present is rooted in two interpretations of
courts. One interpretation leads to *the diversion alternative*,
suggesting that demands for due process and substantive jus-

tice are not fulfilled in lower courts because of abuses in the exercise of judicial discretion. The other interpretation leads to *the dispute-processing alternative*, portraying the structure and function of courts as internally consistent, but unable to handle minor disputes. Each interpretation presents a challenge to formalism as the basis of judicial legitimacy and asserts that the proposed alternatives will mediate the tensions producing a legitimation crisis for courts.

The Diversion Alternative

The various ways in which lower criminal courts are characterized reflect the contradictory roles assigned to them as well as the historic ambivalence toward their performance (Silbey, 1981). Critics chastise these courts for violating the norms of procedural fairness, yet attack the appropriateness of such norms for the type of conflicts routinely channeled through lower courts. The goal of judicial reform is to reconcile these contradictory expectations by creating alternatives to conventional adjudication.

Herbert Packer's (1968) two well known models of the criminal justice system (due process and crime control) depict the tension reformers seek to mediate. They illustrate the contrast between *ideals of fairness* and the demands that lower courts provide *substantive justice* through problem solving. Packer emphasizes that these two models are "an attempt to abstract two separate value systems that compete for priority in the operation of the criminal process. Neither is presented as either corresponding to reality or representing the ideal to the exclusion of the other" (Packer, 1968:153). The judicial reform challenge is to conform judicial practices to both value systems.

Research on police behavior and lower courts, however, suggests that official attitudes and practices toward defendants are best characterized by the values of the crime control model rather than the norms of the due process model. Studies of lower criminal courts describe mass justice or "rapid case processing" as being at odds with the conventional notions of due process justice (Mileski, 1971). This seems to be true despite differences in the political culture of urban courts (Jacob, 1973; Levin, 1977), and the size of the community, disposition style, or sources of case-processing pressure (Alfini and Doan, 1977). Other studies have tried to determine what factors influence the dominance of crime control over due process values. For example, studies of police behavior discuss the impact of professional training and socialization on the style of policing (Wilson, 1968; Skolnick, 1966; Blumberg, 1967; Goldstein, 1977). Criminal court studies focus on the effects of institutional and organizational constraints and the impact of political culture on adjudication styles and sentencing practices in lower courts (Eisenstein and Jacob, 1977; Levin, 1977; Feeley, 1979, Ryan, 1981).[14]

These studies tend to assess the quality of justice in lower courts against the standards of due process. Therefore, evaluations of the conditions in lower courts most often conclude that lower court justice is of an inferior quality—routine "assembly line justice" (Blumberg, 1967; Downie, 1971; Jacob, 1973; Robertson, 1974). Collectively, this research describes a paradox: along with the recognition that lower courts fail to provide substantive justice, there is an unwillingness to abandon the legal theory (formalism) that legitimates institutions decidedly different from lower courts.

The lower court paradox was also embedded in the dominant lower court reform strategy of the late 1960s to the mid–1970s. The dominant strategy embraced the ideals of procedural fairness, yet placed minimal value on the role of these norms in addressing the substantive needs of problem solving. The exercise of discretion by police and prosecutors became the focal point of reform. Reformers observed that the daily decisions about the administration of justice neither conformed to the ideals of procedural fairness nor would it be easy to standardize decision making in the unsupervised decentralized environment of lower courts (Davis, 1969).[15] Discretion, they maintained, posed a threat to judicial legitimacy.

The basic trouble with discretion is simply that it is lawless, in the literal sense of that term. If police or prosecutors find themselves free (or compelled) to pick and choose, they are making judgments which in a society based on law should be made only by those to whom the making of law is entrusted. . . . When victims of discriminatory enforcement see what is happening, secondary effects subversive of respect of law . . . are produced (Davis, 1969:290).

The pre-arrest and pre-trial stages in minor dispute processing were identified as being particularly susceptible to abuses of discretionary authority: "the worst discretion in enforcement occurs in connection with those offenses that are just barely taken seriously . . . it is here that the greatest danger exists of using enforcement discretion in an abusive way" (Ibid.:290–291).

Diversion programs were offered to reconcile conflicting expectations about lower courts and regain institutional legitimacy. The design emphasized controlling the exercise of official discretion through procedural safeguards, while providing individualized justice. Although based on a different interpretation of courts, the diversion alternative established procedural and substantive justifications for the exercise of discretion that would later be incorporated into the alternative dispute resolution alternative.

The procedural justification for diversion programs is that formal guidelines (e.g., age of offender, seriousness of charge, and previous record) limit the scope of official discretion. Restrictions on the exercise of discretion by prosecutors (pre-arrest) and judges (pre-trial and post-conviction sentencing alternative) are pre-conditions for imposing sanctions. Diversion guidelines, the Vorenbergs maintain, provide a "new screening device to select those who will leave" or continue through the courts (Vorenberg and Vorenberg, 1973:152). Indeed, the *ideal* of diversion is an "attempt to structure and make visible the informal prosecutorial practices of noncriminal disposition" (*Yale Law Journal*, 1974:852). This attempt at controlling official discretion, reformers argue, protects individual rights in these situations and thus establishes some semblance of procedural fairness.

The substantive justification for division is rehabilitation. Government support for diversion as an alternative to prosecution was initially affirmed in the 1967 President's Commission on Law Enforcement and the Administration of Justice. It called for "early identification and diversion to other community resources of those offenders in need of treatment, for whom full criminal disposition does not appear required" (*Yale Law Journal*, 1974:8282). In 1973, the Task Force of the National Commission on Criminal Justice Standards and Goals explicitly defined diversion as the "utilization of alternatives to . . . the justice system" (Nimmer, 1974:5). The subjects of diversion fell into two general categories: "(1) persons charged with offenses of dubious or controversial criminality, such as drug use, drunkenness, and juvenile status offenses and (2) persons for whom ordinary criminal processing may be dysfunctional, such as domestic assaulters, misdemeanants, and juveniles" (Robertson, 1972:335).

Early diversion and pre-trial diversion programs were developed as *treatment alternatives* to customary criminal sanctions (see Feeley, 1983: Chapter 3). The origins of this treatment approach stemmed from criminology's courtship with labeling and symbolic interaction theory (Vorenberg and Vorenberg, 1973; Austin, 1977). Both theories drew attention away from thinking about the causes of deviance in terms of an individual's characteristics by shifting the focus to the interactions between offenders and social control agencies. Labeling by the criminal justice system was viewed as contributing to, if not creating, deviant behavior by stigmatizing one as a "deviant." Once criminologists focused on the consequences of labeling behavior, the offender's reactions became an important focus of reform alternatives. As a result of greater sensitivity to the dynamics of defining and creating deviance, closer attention was given to the role of offenders in rehabilitation.

In the area of correctional policy, the Vorenbergs observed that the rehabilitation theory was "the heart of the [Crime] commission's recommendations about prisons" (Vorenberg and Vorenberg, 1973:153). These recommendations called for reforming correctional policy so that prisons would function as "collaborative institutions" (Ibid.). This meant that the "offender should have the privilege/burden of participating in decisions affecting him" (Ibid.). Likewise, in the area of pre-arrest and pre-trial diversion, the Commission's recommendations called for a collaborative approach, which meant increasing the "offender's" role in rehabilitation. Contract-like agreements between the offender and the caseworker were proposed as a way of stimulating participation and encouraging collaboration in sanctioning decisions. Thus, critical to the concept of diversion alternatives was the view that participation produces some form of structured treatment—the substantive justification for alternatives. This emphasis on participation is present in the dispute-processing alternative as well.

Critics of diversion contend that throughout the development of diversion theory multiple goals were articulated: "Avoid costly criminal processing of questionable benefit to the individual and society, while maintaining social control through services aimed at altering behavior" (Robertson, 1972:225). The diversion alternative, they suggest, contains the danger of expanding social control. Instead of restricting official decision making, these programs are "an outlet for existing tendencies" in the exercise of discretion (Nimmer, 1974:96). With the institutionalization of diversion programs, authorities gain control over a broader range of behavior that was essentially noncriminal (Nejelski, 1976; Gorelick, 1975; Nimmer, 1974; *Yale Law Journal*, 1974; Roesch, 1978). Rather than mediating between the values of due process and crime control, the diversion alternative potentially legitimizes the crime control model already in place.

In response, defenders of the diversion alternative emphasize the importance of shared responsibility for checking discretion and for altering behavior. The defenders argued that the expansion of official authority, which might result from the institutionalization of diversion programs, is balanced by the accompanied increase in offenders' participation in the process. The requirement that offenders voluntarily participate in alternatives as well as meet the screening criteria, they argued, are checks on official intervention in pre-arrest and pre-conviction cases (Vorenberg and Vorenberg, 1973; Brakel, 1971; Gottheil, 1979).

Participation by the offender in the process of sanctioning is central to the concept of diversion alternatives. In fact, participation plays a dual role. On the one hand, participation by the offender is thought to reduce official discretion. On the other hand, participation by the offender is viewed as essential in rehabilitating the offender.

The Dispute-Processing Alternative

Whereas the diversion alternative seeks to *mediate* conflicting demands on the lower court, dispute-processing alternatives seek to *eliminate* some of those demands on courts altogether. The second interpretation emphasizes the limited capacity of courts to effectively resolve social problems. This interpretation follows principally from Donald Horowitz's (1977) writings on federal courts, but is made by lower court reformers as well (also see Barton, 1975; Glazer, 1975; Rifkind, 1976; Judicial Conference of the ABA, 1976). Horowitz argues that courts operate best when they function according to the traditional model of judicial decision making. In this model, the judicial method is defined as a process of making decisions on grounds that are general and neutral and "transcend any immediate result that is involved" (Wechsler, 1959:39). The structure of adjudication is confined to judgments about individual rights and does not include the crafting or implementing of remedies and treatments for the parties involved. In sum, courts function effectively for "resolving limited kinds of questions and remedies because of the nature, organization and structure of judicial power" (Halpern, 1978:5).

Horowitz attempts to distinguish his interpretations from previous defenses of the traditional model (Wechsler, 1959) by claiming that his assessment of court capacity is based on an empirical evaluation rather than a normative theory of judicial review in a democracy. Relying on four cases of "judicial activism" (educational equality, juvenile court reform, controlling police behavior, and implementing legislative standards for Model Cities programs), he concludes that in all of these cases the courts lacked the necessary capacity to effectively handle "complex litigation."

Other scholars and judicial reformers have a similar view of minor dispute adjudication (Judicial Conference of the ABA, 1976; Sander, 1976; Johnson et al., 1977). The category "minor disputes" includes civil disputes involving small amounts of money and criminal charges such as simple assault, disorderly conduct, and harassment in cases where the parties know one another.[16] These reformers see inherent limitations in the capacity of lower courts to effectively resolve related party cases (Fuller, 1971; Danzig, 1973; Nader and Singer, 1976; Sander, 1976; Cratsley, 1978, Mnookin and Kornhauser, 1979).

Two claims about the nature of related party cases are central to this argument although not unique to this view: (1) related party cases are complex, and (2) they require a decision-making process that is more flexible than conventional adjudication. Disputants in related party cases, the reformers argue, are often reluctant to take their problems to court. It is suggested that the high percentage of related party court cases that end in dismissals because one party drops out (most often the complainants) indicates that disputants do not feel they will have a significant role in shaping a court resolution. Psychological, economic, and temporal costs together with the linguistic and cultural barriers, reformers say, make courts ineffective mechanisms for processing minor disputes (Galanter, 1974; Johnson, 1978). These barriers limit citizen participation in dispute processing. Further, reformers attribute court avoidance to distrust of the courts.

If you go into any urban area in the country you will find, in particularly low income communities, a high incidence of tolerance [for unresolved conflict] because there is no adequate forum to deal with the problem. No one will use the existing forum . . . because they don't trust it, it does not relate to their needs and it does not, in fact, give them anything (Shonholtz, 1978:135).

Participants have a small role in the process outside of manipulating procedures indirectly through the assistance of counsel (see Galanter, 1974; Nader and Singer, 1976). Judgments of guilt or innocence are imposed on the parties. Reformers believe this formal style of adjudication heightens conflict and further alienates citizens from the judicial system.

Proceduralism per se has not been blamed for causing this

sense of alienation. Rather the barriers to entering the legal system along with a minimal role for the parties in shaping the outcome have been identified as causes for the gap between courts and communities (Johnson, 1978). New procedural mechanisms for building a consensus between courts and communities, such as mediation processes, are seen as a remedy to the alleged popular dissatisfaction with courts (Sander, 1976). In fact, advocates of informal dispute processing claim that there is a popular demand for mediation programs. They contend that because mediation expands the disputants' role in both the process and outcome, disputants prefer mediation to court adjudication.

Delegalization reformers characterize courts as closed institutions, constrained by formal procedures. Although this description may sound as if these reformers have not sat through a morning docket in a lower criminal or civil court, they have. They know that informal court negotiations occur routinely (e.g., plea bargaining, prosecutorial discretion, pre-trial conferences), yet they claim that even these negotiations are restrained by formal procedures. They see social conflicts channeled into a process where communication is distorted by legal structures—structures that do not consider the underlying social and interpersonal aspects of a dispute. The forums that in the past have handled "social" as opposed to "legal" disputes, reformers suggest are weak in advanced industrial society (e.g., churches, schools, private associations; see Galanter, 1974).[17] The breakdown or absence of these private dispute mechanisms creates a vacuum between courts and communities. Reformers think this can be filled by informal public dispute tribunals that are proactive instead of reactive institutions like courts.[18]

Reformers maintain that a proactive dispute process will redress the crisis with court capacity for two reasons: (1) it increases community involvement in the management of everyday conflicts, and (2) it absorbs the mass of unresolved conflicts before they turn into bigger problems. The use of lay citizens as mediators in the neighborhood justice program is one way of engaging the community in the process and giving responsibility to the community for *facilitating* a public problem-solving process. This strategy is much like that of the diversion alternative, where offenders are included in the sanctioning process.

The second attribute of a proactive dispute process is its capacity to prevent and resolve conflict. This is one of the main themes in the ideology of delegalization reform. A proactive dispute process is in fact defined as having the ability to resolve disputes that are hard to regulate directly by law, such as disputes about social behavior (e.g., order maintenance problems). Essentially the argument is that social order is best achieved *without* imposing the force of law and through the active participation of the parties. The claim is that if disputants participate more directly in creating and enforcing agreements, they will last longer than a court order (Nonet and Selznick, 1978; Aaronson et al., 1977; Wahrhaftig, 1978). In short, the most fundamental device for maintaining order is a voluntary process that produces consensus on future behavior (see Shapiro, 1975).

A central assumption of the alternatives movement is that disputes between individuals or groups in "ongoing" relationships can draw on the "capacity to sanction," which is built into these type of relationships (Galanter, 1974:128). Reformers rely on several studies suggesting that the "relational distance" between individuals is the major determinant of adjudication style (Black, 1973; Galanter, 1974; Sarat, 1976). Disputes in ongoing relationships between neighbors, landlord and tenant, consumer and seller, employer and worker, and within families are more likely to use a private informal style of dispute processing.

This interpretation of court capacity, and the dispute-processing alternative that emerges from it, offers a structural functionalist analysis of adjudication and mediation. Formal and informal dispute processes are separated from this social role as dispute processes and each assigned a distinctive function. The relationship between adjudication and mediation is ignored, indeed, they appear to share little although they are both dispute-processing forums.

The dispute-processing alternative substitutes the *disputants' capacity* for the court's. The *structure of mediation*, distinguished from adjudication, enhances the capacity of disputants to reach a consensus on future behavior, because it involves them more directly in the negotiation and the construction of a settlement. The structure of mediation is characterized as being a more congenial environment for expressing underlying issues in conflicts between related parties. *The function of mediation*, reformers maintain, facilitates the resolution of these conflicts by drawing on the sanctions and incentives within the disputants' relationship.

Some scholars have rightly questioned the validity of this court capacity argument as an empirical interpretation of courts and adjudication (see Halpern, 1978, Cavanagh and Sarat, 1980; Shapiro, 1981). Its empirical basis *is* questionable, given the implicit judgments about what is and is not effective dispute resolution. Even further, empirical research on civil litigation "disputes" the assertion that the function of courts is bound to the structure of the traditional model of judicial decision making (Trubek et al, 1983a). Whether the court capacity interpretation is a sound empirical argument or simply presented to us as such to mask its normative bias against judicial intervention in certain kinds of social conflict, it nonetheless represents a *renewed* support for the traditional model (e.g., Judicial Conference of the ABA, 1976; Sander, 1977; Aaronson et al., 1977). This renewed support has influenced renewed efforts to experiment with alternatives to court.

FUNCTIONALISM: THE RESPONSE TO "COURT CRISIS"

The ideology of judicial reform in the Progressive period and today shares a common structure. Although each concept of an alternative may stem from slightly different notions of what constitutes a crisis, informalism is the common solution. The shared framework of alternatives constitutes the new basis for judicial legitimacy and it represents a shift away from reforming rules to reforming results. The new basis of legitimacy for minor dispute processing is treatment through participation in sanctioning. Proceduralism is clearly part of the alterna tives movement (see Garth, 1982), yet the *purpose* of alternative procedures is to reach a consensus on future behavior.

Elements of the ideology of the socializing courts and the more recent diversion alternatives are present in the dispute-processing alternative. The concept of treatment, central to socializing the immigrant and reforming the offender, is essential to restructuring the future behavior of the disputants. Dispute-processing alternatives expand on the themes of collaboration and participation, developed by the Progressives and present in diversion programs, by including both parties in the sanctioning process.

In a democracy, we tend to think that the expansion of popular participation in the judicial system is a progressive advance. Although this may be true, the context of such reforms is more telling than the claim alone. The ideology of this judicial reform is part of the socio-legal context. In the twentieth century that ideology is poltically conservative.[19] The conservatism of this reform is evident in the social relations it constructs. Alternatives are proposed as a solution to political and economic demands (demands for equality and fairness on the one hand and law and order on the other hand), which threaten a traditional definition of court capacity. The design of these alternatives preserves traditional notions of institutional legitimacy (formalism), while crafting an "alternative" rationale to legitimate informal institutions (functionalism).

The ideology of alternatives can be understood as a response to: (1) criticism of lower courts for not providing procedural or substantive justice to minor offenders, and (2) the claim that courts cannot effectively address social demands expressed in complex disputes because such disputes require a more flexible negotiation process that involves the parties more directly in decision making. In response to these criticisms, the concept of alternatives suggests a new basis for legitimacy—functionalism. The legitimacy of the process is measured by its results—its purpose rather than its standards of procedural fairness. The problem-solving orientation of functionalism, in contrast to formalism, places a special emphasis on the importance of participation. Participation is viewed as a key factor in altering behavior and establishing a long lasting consensus. It is also seen as reducing alienation and popular dissatisfaction with courts, and therefore increasing the willingness of disputants to use public informal dispute processes. Functionalism expands the institutional capacity of the judicial system by incorporating resources and capacities of disputants.

CONCLUSION

The ideals of informalism present a picture of the state withdrawing its authority over minor dispute management, and a proactive community mediation process providing a therapeutic context for dispute resolution. This examination of the sociological foundations of informalism suggests that this is not the case. State authority is not withdrawing from dispute resolution in periods of informal reform, it is being transformed. Nonet and Selznick suggest that as "the legal system expands its critical resources, it delegates more discretion to decide what is authoritative. Legal participation takes on new meaning; it also extends to the making and interpretation of legal policy" (Nonet and Selznick, 1978:95).

As new resources are incorporated into the management of conflict,[20] the role of state actors in this effort is critical to the politics of this reform. The state's role and interest in integrating participation in order maintenance should not be underplayed. Forms of therapeutic intervention in conflict resolution often blur the state's role in *organizing* those forums for building consensus and in *defining* what conflicts they will hear.

NOTES

1. Whether or not court reforms are needed or dissatisfaction is widespread, the banality of attacks on lower courts, which underly reform, has had an effect on the creation of institutions and the generation of expectations. For a more elaborate treatment of this point see Murray Edelman's work on political language. In his vivid analysis of how banal political language structures social meaning he argues that:

In politics, as in religion, whatever is ceremonial or banal strengthens reassuring beliefs regardless of their validity and discourages skeptical inquiry about disturbing issues. . . . Governments have won the support of large numbers of their citizens for policies that were based upon delusions: beliefs in witches, in nonexistent internal and external enemies, or in the efficacy of laws to regulate private power, cope with destitution, guarantee civil rights, or rehabilitate criminals that have often had the opposite effect from their intended ones (Edelman, 1977:3).

2. Although this chapter focuses on delegalization reforms in the twentieth century, it should be noted that between 1846 and 1851 conciliation procedures were inserted in several state constitutions. Commenting on the failure of those conciliation courts, Boston writes: "The constitution of 1846 in New York provided for the institution of a Court of Conciliation, but the time did not seem to have been ripe and it became a dead letter, to be eliminated in 1894" (Boston, 1917:111; also see Smith, 1919b:61, 1926:40; and Vance, 1917). Also see Auerbach's discussion of the Freedmen's Bureau, a federal agency established after the Civil War to settle civil disputes. Auerbach argues that "in the second half of the nineteenth century, the purpose (if not the forms) of alternative dispute settlement were redefined. Fears of racial discord and class warfare injected arbitration as a remedy for the congestive breakdown of the court system and as an externally imposed deterrent to social conflict. Until the Civil War alternative dispute settlement expressed an ideology of community justice. Thereafter, as it collapsed into an argument for judicial efficiency it became an external instrument of social control" (Auerbach, 1983:57).

3. Formalism is the traditional legal theory used to legitimate and distinguish judicial institutions from other decision-making bodies. See Kennedy (1973), Unger (1976), and Nonet and Selznick (1978) for a description of legal formalism and institutional legitimacy.

4. See Feeley (1976) for a discussion of the problems with gap studies. For an example of a gap analysis of the neighborhood justice movement see Tomasic (1982).

5. Robert Gordon argues that "evolutionary functionalism" has also been the dominant tradition in legal history. "Formalism" and "Realism" have "worked out contrasting visions of what social development consists of and how law has adapted to that development," according to Gordon, but "without disturbing the fundamental assumption of progressive adaptation that they hold in common" (Gordon, 1984:66). This tradition shares the *a priori* perspective in common with other functionalist views of legal ideology. In Munger

and Seron's study (1984) a similar point is made in the context of sociological research beyond the Critical Legal Studies movement. For further discussion of the study of legal ideology see Klare (1979) and Brigham (1984). See also Hunt (1985) for a discussion of the "concrete model" of legal ideology. This model, he suggests, will allow us to integrate questions about relative autonomy of law and determinism by focusing on the "effectivity" of law.

6. Marc Galanter makes a similar observation in his analysis of disputes. "Disputes and knowledge about disputes [are] kindred social constructions" (Galanter, 1983:61).

7. This distinction between judicial power and judicial authority is the difference between jurisdiction and legitimacy.

8. Historians have given considerable attention to the question of who supported Progressivism. Samuel Hays notes that "reformers maintained that their movement rested on a wave of popular demands, calling their gatherings of business and professional leaders 'mass meetings,' . . . [and describing] their reforms as 'part of a worldwide trend toward popular government'" (Hays, 1964:167; see also Hofstadter, 1955:Chs. 4–7; Lasch, 1965:Ch. 6; Wiebe, 1967). Similarly, Progressives characterized reforms proposed by Bar associations and trade associations as expressions of popular discontent.

9. Judge Ransom was referring to the development of public service commissions, commerce commissions, and railroad commissions.

10. In the literature on conflict resolution, scholars have been careful to make a distinction between dispute resolution and dispute processing. Analytically, that distinction notes the difference between reaching a settlement or resolving a conflict and processing a claim without resolving it. The term "alternative dispute resolution" is used here with less precision. It has become one of the many ways of referring to the contemporary reform movement.

11. Bruce Mann's (1984) research on arbitration practices before the American Revolution documents the impact of changing social contexts on arbitration awards. He states: "The key lies in the community nexus of arbitration. Arbitration in Connecticut before the end of the seventeenth century was deeply rooted in the communities it served. . . . What worked for members of the same community, however, did not necessarily work for others. The social context of disputing changed as population growth and migration weakened the cohesiveness of existing towns and as new towns were settled by individuals [land speculators] rather than by groups [migration of villages from England or congregations of religious dissenters]" (Ibid.:480). His analysis of the 1753 Connecticut arbitration statute

suggests that it transformed both the content (substantive formalization) and form (procedural formalization) of arbitration awards. For a historical description of early commercial arbitration see Auerbach (1983:33).

12. For a general survey of legal developments in this period, see Hurst (1956) and Horowitz (1977). Wolfe (1977:Ch. 3–4) provides a summary of the transition from merchant to corporate capitalism and the development of the state. Also see Lustig (1982) and Skowronek (1982).

13. Galanter takes the position that the charge of "litigiousness" is unique to the contemporary reform. He says that: "Earlier reformers, addressing themselves to problems of overloaded courts, high costs, and delay, saw the problems in terms of institutional failure rather than of excessive use of the courts. But for these earlier commentators, the problem was one of poorly designed and managed institutional machinery rather than of inappropriate and insatiable demands upon that machinery" (Galanter, 1983:7, footnote 7).

14. Ethnographies of lower courts provide another way of understanding the dynamics of local culture and court ideology in the context of dispute processing. See Yngvesson (1985) and Merry (1985).

15. In part because of the unsupervised nature of lower courts and the "discovery" that conditions in lower courts were very poor, the President's Commission on Law Enforcement and Administration of Justice (1967) recommended that misdemeanor courts be abolished as separate entities and merge them with felony courts under the unification model for state courts. In 1973, government agencies again recommended unification as a method for solving the problems with misdemeanor courts (see National Advisory Commission on Criminal Justice Standards and Goals—Task Force on Courts, 1973; also see Chapter 2 for a discussion of unification).

16. See Griffith (1969) for a discussion of the changing definitions and meanings of what is "criminal" under the "family model" of dispute processing. Also see Aaronson et al., (1977) and Sander (1976).

17. For a discussion of the viability of mediation in contemporary industrial societies see the debate between Danzig and Lowy (1975) and Felstiner (1974 and 1975). Also see Merry (1979).

18. Proactive refers to an active style of third party intervention or setting (see Black, 1973; Baum et al., 1976).

19. See Abel (1981) for a discussion of delegalization and the construction of conservative approaches to conflict resolution.

20. The grass roots citizen dispute resolution reformers see media-

tion as a form of organizing and empowering the community (see Chapter 3). Their approach to community mediation is embedded in concepts of community development (Wahrhaftig, 1982; and Christie, 1977), rather than judicial reform (Johnson, 1978).

Part II

ORGANIZING LEGAL RESOURCES

CHAPTER TWO

Judicial Management and Delegalization

A more diverse range of disputes are now being targeted as candidates for informalism than in the Progressive period (see Chapter 3). In both periods, however, special attention has been given to constructing tribunals for managing everyday disputes, or what might be called *order maintenance problems*. Order maintenance is a term that refers to a style of intervention by officials or a type of "control system" (Mileski, 1971:481). Conflict is handled informally on a case-by-case basis rather than by the enforcement of legal standards (see Wilson, 1968; Goldstein, 1977). I also use the term to describe the kind of conflicts most often subject to this style of official dispute treatment. These conflicts include disorderly conduct, disturbing the peace, and simple assault and battery.

Reformers have focused on these types of social conflicts in part because they believe that the "sporting theory of justice," as Pound referred to formality, is particularly flawed in "petty causes." The expense to both the parties and the state of observing procedural rights, they argue, is prohibitive and thereby the process frustrates the exercise of individual rights and the efficient management of conflict. Attention to the costs of procedural justice, however, is not unique to minor disputes. Financial barriers have long been recognized as a major constraint in many types of cases. What *is* most striking about these two periods of reform is that order maintenance problems are *channeled* and *absorbed* into specialized forums.

The intention of this chapter is not to determine whether delegalization reforms have adequately resolved the problems identified with legal formalism. Rather, I will argue that the delegalization of minor dispute processing occurs within the context of a broader social reform: *the construction in the Progressive period and reconstruction today of a rationality for judicial management of lower court organization and for intervention in everyday conflicts.* Further, I argue that the architecture of judicial management outlines the institutional boundaries of judicial reform. This is as true for the alternatives movement today as it was for informal reforms in the Progressive period. Although the contemporary organization and administration of justice differs in subtle ways, the architecture of judicial management continues to provide a key to understanding the politics of informalism. This is so for two related reasons. Informalism is both a product of the changing character of court organization and administration, and in both periods it is essential to the process of implementing management strategies.

Despite the fact that some critics today vigorously oppose the view that justice means "efficient service," management has been a key characteristic of informalism and not merely a flawed by-product. The style and structure of management strategies shape the politics of informalism. These strategies are also dependent on the ideology of informalism for institutional legitimation.[1] Although strategies of judicial management may not be coherent, "uni-directional," or "uni-dimensional" (Heydebrand, 1979:30), they do reflect a mode of rationalization for both the *adjudication process* and the *judicial work process* in courts.[2] Specifically, I will argue that the mode of rationalization associated with delegalization reforms is an administrative-technocratic approach to the organization of the judicial work process and the management of order maintenance problems in urban poor and working-class communities.

THE RISE OF JUDICIAL MANAGEMENT AND INFORMALISM

The judicial reorganization movement beginning in the late 1880s created an environment for experimentation with informal procedures for handling minor disputes. It may seem ironic that the same group of Progressive reformers who led the battle against Justice of the Peace (JP) Courts advocated the use of simplified procedures, arbitration, and conciliation for processing minor disputes. The "khadi-justice" of the justices courts was transformed under the Progressive movement into "socialized law." What accounts for the simultaneous hostility toward JP courts and zealous support of informal procedures?

It is difficult to generalize about the caseload and dispositions of Justice of the Peace Courts between 1890 and 1930. Their jurisdictions were so diverse: most were not courts of record, and researchers did not use uniform methods to collect and report data. Nonetheless, the literature is replete with generalizations about outcomes: 80 percent of the cases were default judgments, the court's nickname—"judgment for the plaintiff"—was a consequence of the fee system (Schramm, 1928; Keebler, 1930; Douglass, 1932; Howard, 1935; Blackburn, 1935; Vanlandingham, 1964; Ireland, 1972). It is striking that most of this literature focuses on the organization and outcomes of these courts rather than on the type of cases they heard or the procedures they followed. The irregularities in procedure are attributed to their decentralized organization. Herbert Harley, founder and secretary of the American Judicature Society (1913), described the evils of decentralization.

Our present inferior court systems exemplify our powerful inclination toward decentralization. They are courts of and for the people living in town and country. The fact that they are democratic is no valid excuse for inefficiency. It is an unfriendly ideal of democracy which excludes *efficient service*. Democracy like every other ideal, must justify itself by its works (Harley, 1917a:190; emphasis added).

Reformers such as Harley believed the Justice of the Peace Courts failed to provide an efficient service not so much because summary procedures and informal negotiations predominated, but because they lacked administration.[3] Those calling for the abolition of the JP courts objected to their decentralized organization, the high degree of local autonomy, and the unchecked expansion of their jurisdiction by the legislature (Strasburger, 1915; Wickersham Commission, 1974). At first Harley criticized the lack of administrative control rather than the qualifications of the personnel: "The fact that he [the justice of the peace] is a layman will be no objection [under the unified court proposal] because he will be guided by his responsible superior" (Harley, 1917a:190).

As the movement to organize municipal courts grew and attacks on justices of the peace intensified, the lack of *supervision* was the main weapon against these courts. The call for greater supervision came to include a demand for professional training.

Argument against an inferior class of judges to serve a lower salary has been submitted. There are certain duties, however, more administrative than judicial, which can properly be performed by an official of lower salary under the direction of a judge. To meet this need the act should provide for a certain number of *masters*, and fix their compensation. The powers which they shall exercise should be determined by the judicial council. Genuine judicial talent is too rare and too valuable to be permitted to wear itself out on details which can as well be done by an assistant. Masters may become highly expert, and as long as they are directed, may prove economical from more than the mere financial standpoint (Harley, 1915a:513; emphasis added).

During this period of institutional transformation and expansion of the legal profession (see Larson, 1977), the legal profession sought to distinguish its role from the duties of justices of the peace by describing their functions as administrative instead of judicial. This type of distinction contributed to a growing trend toward the stratification of decision making into administrative and judicial categories.

Charges that Justice of the Peace Courts were corrupt stemmed in large part from the fact that the justices were paid a proportion of the fines they collected (Kogan, 1974:110). Following the Supreme Court's decision in *Tumey v. Ohio* (273 U.S. 510, 1927) that the fee system was unconstitutional in criminal cases, reformers hoped the JP courts would be abolished. In many states, however, that required a constitutional amendment. To avoid lengthy and difficult procedure, reformers passed legislation giving the newly formed municipal courts the same jurisdiction as the Justice of the Peace Courts. But this strategy had no impact in rural areas, and in some urban areas it also proved ineffective (Douglass, 1932).

Although all reformers clearly felt that the more serious disputes were denied justice in JP courts because formal rules were not applied, Pound (1913) and others nonetheless argued that the "petty litigants" were hurt by formality. Pound contended that eliminating pleadings and rules of evidence and allowing disputants to submit their responses by mail would permit access to a higher quality of justice. The American Bar Association Special Committee to Suggest Remedies and Formulate Proposed Laws to Prevent Delay and Unnecessary Cost in Litigation wrote about the Chicago Municipal Court: "It is perfectly feasible to administer a much *higher grade of justice* in petty causes than that dispensed by the justice of the peace *without resort to the* cumbrous and expensive machinery of our *superior courts* of record" (American Bar Association, 1909:591; emphasis added).

Professionalism served to justify supervision of minor dispute processing by expanding the definition of what was "professional" to include administrative tasks. Terence Halliday's history of the Chicago Bar Association demonstrates that professional expansionism depended on "the capacity of the profession to exert control over its primary sphere of institutional activity and to extend its influence into various secondary spheres" (Halliday, 1979:13). This capacity is a "direct result of a profession's accomplishments in dressing its normative contributions to change in technical clothes" (Ibid.). Similarly, professionals sought to supplant the Justice of the Peace Courts by presenting the managerial solution to the problem of lower court organization as a process of democratization.

Whether "efficient service" under the supervision of profes-

sionals represented an increase in democracy or not has been
a subject of much debate. The more interesting point, however, is the central paradox of this period of municipal reform:
"the ideology of an extension of political control and the practice of its concentration" (Hays, 1964:167). The municipal court
movement (1904–1930), like the pervasive municipal reform
movement, expanded the role of experts in the delivery of state
services as well as the scope of those services (see Schiesl, 1977).
This required the reorganization and stratification of the judicial work process, which effected dispute-processing methods.

The principles that structured this movement were largely
derived from the influential model of scientific management.
The principles of scientific management, first developed in
factories (Braverman, 1974; Burawoy, 1979; Edwards, 1979;
Clawson, 1980), were understood by court reformers as "capable of being applied to any given form of human activity"
(Jessup, 1917:4). The American Judicature Society, state and
local Bar associations, and private trade associations all agreed
on the importance of the scientific model of efficiency. Frederick Taylor's theory of scientific management (1911) was explicitly adopted in early reorganization proposals as *the* cure
for the crisis of the courts. In one of their debates on judicial
reform, a group of New York City lawyers, the Phi Delta Phi
Club's Committee on Nine, proposed that courts be organized
and managed like any other business.

Treating the system of administrating justice as if it were a great
machine, it is obvious that if the courts are to be regulated by the
same theories of efficiency as any other administrative business or
organization, what we desire must be a frictionless movement of a
well-lubricated machine in which all the parts cooperate to produce
the desired result. "Peace" in its last analysis is frictionless activity,
not inaction of human life . . . [it is] the ultimate desired condition
of the administration of justice, in spite of the fact that the administration of justice relates itself to the settlement of contentious disputes (Jessup, 1917:4).

Pound asserted that the concept of efficiency was necessary "in
a modern court no less than in a modern factory" (Pound,

1940b:286). The application of scientific management to the judicial work process increased centralization and specialization.

Court unification was the instrument through which the principles of scientific management were implemented. Thus in court reform, as in municipal reform, power was concentrated through the unification of the courts. The ideology of "efficient service" suggested that access to justice was being extended to those who most frequently came in contact with lower courts—the powerless.

A UNIFIED JUDICIAL SYSTEM

Pound was the first American to advocate a unified judicial system on the ground that the prevailing decentralized structure could not respond to the demands of a growing industrialized urban population. Relying on the English model of unification developed in 1873, he called for the consolidation of all state appellate and trial courts into a single structure with two layers (Pound, 1906). In 1940, he modified this model by including an additional tier of minor trial courts (Ashman and Parness, 1974; Berkson and Carbon, 1978). An ABA report on the administration of justice in 1909 outlined principles of unification similar to those suggested by Pound. In 1920, at the request of the American Judicature Society, the National Municipal League drafted a model state judicial unification proposal (see Berkson and Carbon, 1978:5). The National Economic League of Boston and the Phi Delta Phi Club of New York City (a group of lawyers studying professional problems) were some of the other groups urging the adoption of a unified court organization (Jessup, 1917). All of these proposals were concerned with the organization of entire state judicial systems. These procedural and managerial reforms directly affected the operation of lower courts (see Vanderbilt, 1955; Elliott, 1959; Galub, 1968). Indeed, when Pound announced his unification proposal (1906) he applauded the first municipal court (Chicago, 1904) for adopting managerial and procedural innovations together with the principles of unification.

Managing the Judicial Work Process

Before examining the impact of these principles on the establishment of specific tribunals, a brief overview of the management concepts and procedural reforms helps to explain the
relationship between court reorganization and the implementation of informal procedures. The most significant development was the centralization of management through the creation of a *presiding judge* in the municipal court. This
established a single judicial officer empowered to supervise
record keeping, control case load, and "clerical subordinates"
(Cohen, 1917; *JAJS*, 1928; Willoughby, 1929:339–340). The
introduction of a *unified calendar* regulating case load enhanced the administrative power of the presiding judge. Earlier attempts to control local courts through reorganization
alone failed because of the "political power of clerks and mar-
shals" (*JAJS*, 1928:117). Reformers had always viewed clerks
as "partially independent functionaries over whom courts [had]
little real control" (American Bar Association, 1909:591). It was
not until 1928 that the presiding judges in most municipal
courts were given the authority to manage their staffs and
control calendars.

The calendar system of case load management also introduced specialization. Even before judges came to view themselves as specialists, dockets were specialized to maximize the
efficiency of each judge. Specialized tribunals—small claims,
domestic relations—were also developed as branches of the
municipal court. Describing the virtues of specialized tribunals, Harley compared the management of courts with business
principles of management:

Not to have specialization and direction would be equivalent, in the
business world, to employing fifty or one hundred clerks for a department store and allowing them to do any part of the work which
they might, at any time, prefer to do. . . . In commercial terms, our
judicial business is done at a number of small and disassociated shops
(Harley, 1915a:516).

Each branch was headed by a presiding judge who performed
management tasks similar to those of the judge.

Although reformers adopted specialization as a strategy for rationalizing organization, they did so cautiously. Harley warned: "Specialization is the demand of the times, but *unification should precede specialization.* Without an overhead organization specialization means a new form of waste" (Harley, 1917b:23). Unification antedated specialization, introducing principles of efficiency into both the work process of courts and dispute resolution procedures. To respond to the lack of coordination resulting from the growth of specialization, reformers argued that courts needed greater authority to regulate these developments. Proposals for judicial rule making and for allowing municipal court judges to create specialized tribunals expanded judicial autonomy. At the same time that the Bar was proposing judicial self-regulation as an alternative to citizen-initiated petitions to recall judges (see Cohen, 1917; Potter, 1922:166; McKean, 1963:Ch. 5; Kogan, 1974), lawyers argued that greater judicial autonomy from legislative oversight would lead to the adoption of efficient administration and the virtues of scientific management.

On the one hand, this expansion of judicial autonomy legitimated the exercise of discretion by lower court judges, who could now establish specialized tribunals and adopt informal procedures through judicial rule making. On the other hand, the rise of court management stratified judicial personnel, creating management posts and dividing work into specialized calendars and tribunals. Power was thus centralized and decentralized at the same time, a recurring phenomenon that seems to accompany informalism. Within this context, the adjudication process was rationalized. In a letter proposing the organization of what would later become the American Judicature Society, Harley wrote: "We may beneficially modify our doctrine of contentious procedure by increasing discretion and responsibility of the court and thus relatively decreasing the importance of advocacy. A trend in this direction appears inevitable" (Harley, 1912a:8).

The Municipal Court Movement

The Chicago Municipal Court served as *the* model for reforming the "old" municipal courts[4] and establishing unified city courts. Through the work of a committee, headed by the mayor and two leading industrialists,[5] the Municipal Court Act was drafted and the Illinois constitution amended, and the municipal court opened in 1906 (Gilbert, 1928; Kogan, 1974). The same constitutional amendment abolished the Justice of the Peace Courts, but most municipal courts were created by legislation, which often meant that the municipal and JP courts had overlapping jurisdictions. Where the legislature could restrict the jurisdiction of the latter (as in Columbus, Ohio and Philadelphia, in 1913) they transferred it to the municipal courts. With few exceptions (such as Kansas City), most municipal courts established between 1904 and 1922 assumed the jurisdiction of police courts over misdemeanors and the arraignment of felonies. Their civil jurisdiction included tort claims under $1,000 and unlimited jurisdiction over contract claims (see Anderson, 1916).

Although reformers agreed that the "modern" city court should be unified, there was some conflict over the scope of unification and the extent of professional control. The most common criticism was that some municipal courts lacked complete jurisdiction over criminal cases. According to the 1917 report on "Unification of Local Government in Chicago" by the Chicago Bureau of Public Efficiency, the most serious short-coming of the municipal court was the failure to establish a "single court to have general charge of the administration of justice" (Willoughby, 1929:287). Efforts to expand the jurisdiction of the municipal court consolidating city and county courts were turned down by Chicago voters in 1922. The Detroit Records Court (1920) was praised as the first successful integration of all criminal jurisdiction in a single court.

Most municipal court judges had to be members of the Bar, usually for five years, and a resident of the city. The first requirement enhanced the control of the relatively young local Bar associations over who would be nominated (Kogan, 1974). Despite heated debates over the virtues of appointed judges, most municipal judges were elected on nonpartisan ballots.

Chicago also provided the model for the creation of branches within the municipal court. Six were established between 1911 and 1916: the Court of Domestic Relations, Speeder's Branch,

Morals Court, Boys Court, Small Claims Court, and the Psychopathic Laboratory. These increased specialization and the division of labor. Harley commented:

> They [branches] succeed because the age demands economical production, and has no reverence for empty formalism, the kind exhibited when a supreme court writes *finis* on a cause after all the original litigants are dead. These new tribunals throw to the wind the rules of evidence, because under our jury and appellate system the knotty subject refuses to be reformed (Harley, 1917b:25).

The application of criteria of efficiency to the reorganization of tribunals for minor disputes under a unified administrative system produced the municipal court and its specialized branches. These courts were designed to respond to two demands: efficient production and legal socialization. How was the rationalization of judicial organization tied to the rationalization of informal procedures for handling minor disputes?

The Socialized Courts

The domestic relations, small claims, and conciliation courts were called "socialized courts" in the sense that their "procedures and remedies focused on diagnosis, prevention, cure, education" (Hurst, 1953:5). Progressives claimed that the specialized tribunals provided "social justice" in contrast to "legal justice," and the denial of justice that occurred if there was no judicial intervention. It was in this sense that the reformers saw informal procedures as delegalizing minor dispute processing.

The idea of socialized courts was introduced in the late 1880s by the juvenile court movement (Faust and Brantingham, 1974:145–149). Juvenile courts developed investigative mechanisms to identify social facts about an individual and apply them in the adjudication process. Probation and parole officers, social workers, and psychopathic clinics were used to diagnose the cause of delinquency. Individuals' dossiers served as the basis for a treatment-oriented disposition. "The end sought [must be the] adjustment of a social difficulty rather than the punishment or penalization of the defendant" (Willoughby, 1929:325).

The juvenile court movement was anti-legal in the sense that it "encouraged minimum procedural formality and maximum dependency on extra-legal resources" (Platt, 1969:141). The juvenile court was more than an instrument for assigning guilt; it was conceptualized as part of a social process capable of adjudicating, preventing, and resolving conflict.

The use of "unofficial" dockets in juvenile courts reflected the belief that children could be treated more effectively through informal dispositions (Ryerson, 1978:93; Rothman, 1980:249–260). There were two main consequences of such unofficial treatment. First, judicial supervision of children expanded. By deemphasizing issues of guilt and innocence, the category of disputes heard in the juvenile court was broadened. "Pre-delinquent" children formed a new group as a result of blurring distinctions between dependent, delinquent, and neglected children (Fox, 1970; Ryerson, 1978:45–46). Second, the "policing machinery" of unofficial treatment "removed many distinctions between the enforcement and adjudication of laws" (Platt, 1969:140). Social workers and psychologists provided new resources for handling juveniles and linked courts to social agencies.[6] The state, represented by probation and parole officers, was cast in the role of "friend," helping poor and working-class immigrant children to become socialized or "Americanized" (Ibid.:139). Both developments rendered the courts more interventionist.

Prior to the establishment of domestic relations courts, police and legal aid attorneys had used conciliation to deal with domestic disputes. As early as 1905, Cleveland had set up a diversion program known as the "Sunrise Court" to handle drunkenness and other petty offenses affecting domestic relations. Under the direction of the famous reformist police chief, Fred Kohler, police negotiated early release from jail in exchange for pre-trial admission of guilt in "the Sunrise Court." Another reform Kohler instituted, the "Golden Rule Policy," encouraged officers to "use their kindly efforts to mediate domestic disputes rather than settle them by arrests" (Walker, 1980:141; see also 1977). Legal aid attorneys mediated domestic disputes as well. Smith attributed the use of conciliation to the attorneys' predisposition *"against* litigation unless it is absolutely necessary" (Smith, 1928:64). Smith further noted that legal aid societies were "able to care for [a] vast volume of business [150,000 cases per year] only because they adjust and conciliate a great proportion of the cases entrusted to them" (Ibid.). New York Municipal Court Judge Edgar Lauer, in a speech to the Association of the Bar of the City of New York, urged that more research be done on conciliation techniques by studying legal aid work (Lauer, 1929:8); and the Legal Aid Work Committee of the American Bar Association did in fact do so.

Domestic Relations Courts

Domestic relations courts (1910–1920) represent the institutionalization of informal dispute processing. Upon the recommendation of the New York State Probation Commission, the first domestic relations court was established in Buffalo in 1910. This court, like most, was created through the rule-making authority of the municipal court. Domestic relations courts adopted the juvenile court philosophy of social justice and applied it to cases of wife abandonment, illegitimacy, failure to support, offenses against minors, and custody disputes.[7] Judge Charles W. Hoffman of Cincinnati, a leading figure in the movement for domestic relations courts, contended that social evidence was more relevant than legal evidence to the goal of rehabilitation in cases such as nonsupport (Zunser, 1926).

The movement to create psychopathic clinics for the municipal court accompanied the establishment of domestic relations courts. Dr. Louise Stevens Bryant, head of the Department of Research and Statistics of the Philadelphia Municipal Court, established the first department of diagnosis and treatment. After studying 6,000 cases from the Domestic Relations Division, she concluded that "while the main issue arising in Courts of Domestic Relations is an economic one, the conditioning factors are physical, mental and social" (Bryant, 1918:198). In addition to developing psychopathic clinics, reformers adopted two strategies to respond to what Dr. Bryant called "conditioning factors": consolidation of domestic relations and juvenile cases in a single family court and the use of conciliation techniques to "maintain the integrity of the family" (Zunser, 1926). Both were part of the reform movement to rationalize procedure and judicial administration.

In many cities juvenile and domestic relations courts had overlapping jurisdictions. This resulted in duplication of services and hindered the use of more comprehensive treatment-oriented dispositions, both of which reformers saw as inefficient administration. Pound (1912; 1940a) called for the centralization of "treatment" in a family court (see also Zunser, 1926; Day, 1928). In 1914, by an amendment to the juvenile court law, the Cincinnati Domestic Relations Court became the first court to have jurisdiction over both types of cases (Blackburn, 1935). Reformers maintained that the centralized family court offered an alternative to the divorce courts organized for the purpose of separating families. Conciliation was presented as *the* alternative feature. The flexibility of conciliation procedures facilitated social investigation into family problems.

As the domestic relations courts have applied themselves to the fast growing problem of desertion and non-support they have more and more employed the method of conciliation. The interest of the state in these cases is that homes should not be broken up except for grave causes and the families should be reunited whenever possible. A litigious proceeding is destructive, it is calculated to embitter the contestants, and after a trial in open court husband and wife feel a real grievance toward each other where before there may have been only a temporary discontent. A conciliation proceeding gives the court its only chance to repair, reunite, and construct (Smith, 1919b:80).

The lack of records on unofficial dispositions prevents us from determining the actual number of cases conciliated. It is also difficult to estimate what proportion of those cases would *not* have gone to court prior to the use of conciliation by the police and legal aid societies. There is a similar paucity of data on unofficial dispositions in domestic relations courts. Smith reported:

Conciliation is used very generally by domestic relations courts as a sort of preliminary proceeding, particularly in Chicago, Philadelphia, and Kansas City. In Cleveland a special division of the Court of Common Pleas, where divorce matters are heard, is in contemplation. Where the domestic relations courts have been given civil jurisdiction, as in Cincinnati and Detroit, they have extended the use of conciliation to the civil proceedings of divorce and separate support (Smith, 1919b:81).

Other accounts of domestic relations courts confirm Smith's observation that conciliation was used as a preliminary procedure, particularly during the initial interviews with the parties. But it is apparent that reformers defined conciliation as almost any attempt by a court official (clerk, prosecutor, judge) to get the parties to resolve their differences, whether at the filing of the complaint, the interviews, or the informal hearing.

This broad definition of conciliation reflected the view that court personnel should play a *proactive* role in the socialized courts. Situations for exercising discretion became opportunities for reconciling disputants on the premise that the objectives of conciliation were "spreading the practice of peaceful settlement of disputes and . . . aiding in overcoming the delays of the law" (Lauer, 1929:4). In many respects, conciliation became a shibboleth to justify the exercise of discretion. Reformers idealized the role of the judge adjudicating minor disputes in lower courts as one of "umpire," although studies of these lower courts reveal a very different picture (Wickersham Commission, 1974). The judge in the socialized courts was to be an "impartial investigator into the truth. He is not a passive agent waiting for objections, he is in affirmative control of the whole proceedings . . . [he] is equipped and empowered not only to prevent injustice but to do justice" (Committee on Small Claims and Conciliation Procedure of the Conference of Bar Association Delegates, quoted in Willoughby, 1929:317). Reformers defined the boundaries of delegalization not by articulating the fine lines between conciliation, mediation, arbitration, and litigation, but by establishing different institutions for minor disputes.[8]

Small Claims Courts and Conciliation Tribunals

We can obtain a clearer understanding of the boundaries of delegalization by examining the debate among reformers over small claims courts and conciliation tribunals. The first small claims court was created in 1913 as a result of what Judge Manuel Levine of Cleveland characterized as the success of earlier experiments with conciliation in the policy prosecutors' office.[9] The Small Claims Court was established by a rule of the Cleveland Municipal Court, which provided in very general language that the "judge shall endeavor to effect an amicable adjustment" (Smith, 1919b:63). In practice, the clerk for the Conciliation Branch initiated the process, offering a settlement to the defendant by either telephone or mail. If that attempt failed, the case would then go before a legally trained judge in the Conciliation Branch. The original rule required the clerk to place all cases involving claims under $35 on the docket of the Conciliation Branch, but this was amended to give discretion to the plaintiff. In 1914, 42 percent of the cases docketed were settled by conciliation, and 23 percent in 1915. In the remainder of the cases, the Conciliation Branch rendered a judgment (Smith, 1919b:63). The court process used simplified procedures, required no pleadings, and cost only a nominal fee of seventy-five cents. Lawyers were discouraged from participating, but not excluded.

Most of the city-wide small claims courts were modeled after Cleveland: Chicago (1916), Minneapolis (1917), New York (1917), and Philadelphia (1920). All were branches of the municipal court, created by a court rule, and their jurisdiction was subject to regulation by the municipal judges. The Kansas legislature, by contrast, created Small Debtors' Courts in Topeka, Leavenworth, and Kansas City in 1913. The act provided that the "board of county commissioners or mayor [select] as judge some reputable resident citizen of approved integrity who is sympathetically inclined to consider the situation of the poor, friendless and misfortunate" (Smith, 1919b:4). The lay judge served without pay and was free to hold court in his own home or place of business, or in a location specified by those who appointed him. The court's jurisdiction was limited to claims under $20 and the law provided that the judge and the defendant should work together to arrange for the payment of the judgment (Edholm, 1915:30).

The Kansas Small Debtors' Court was attacked as representing too "violent" a reaction to the problems of formality that plagued traditional procedures (Smith, 1919b:44). Smith and other prominent reformers opposed this type of conciliation tribunal because it subverted the principle of a unified judicial system. It was criticized on three grounds. First, instead of being organized and supervised by the municipal court, it was independent. Reformers argued that the jurisdiction of the Small Claims Courts had to be supervised by the judiciary rather than by the legislature to ensure sufficient flexibility and planning. Second, reformers objected to the lay judge who provided "justice according to individual conscience after the manner of an Eastern Cadi" (Ibid.:45). Pound also rejected the lay justice in Small Debtors' Court: "The old idea of justice without law administered on the basis of sympathy repeated a feature of the system which failed to be justified by experience. There were no provisions for effective control over the supervision of the tribunal" (Pound, 1940b:268).[10] Finally, reformers criticized the statute for prohibiting attorneys from "intermeddl[ing]" in the process. William Willoughby, director of the Institute for Government Research, commented:

To prohibit the attorney by absolute fiat we consider a mistake. While reiterating the proposition that in most small claims court cases the attorney has no function to perform, we believe that there are likely to be some cases where a party is ignorant, or frightened, or unfamiliar with our language, so that an attorney (the attorney of a legal aid society, for e.g.) might assist the court and facilitate the hearing (Willoughby, 1929:319).

In 1919, after the establishment of municipal small claims courts, the American Judicature Society drafted a model bill to create statewide courts. Although the bill was designed to address the "failures" of the only existing statewide law (North Dakota, 1913) it expressed a general program for the delegalization of minor dispute processing. Two of its central features became the major issues of debate in this period of reform: delegating supervision over the conciliation boards to the trial judge and fixing the jurisdiction of the board. Any voter was eligible to become a conciliator, even a lawyer, although legal training was not required. The American Judicature Society believed that eligibility criteria should be flexible to give the supervising judges maximum discretion. Therefore, they had authority to delay a court hearing in any civil action until the parties tried to reach a settlement with the assistance of a conciliator. If they were unable to do so, the conciliator could arbitrate with the written consent of the parties (*JAJS*, 1919a).

Both of these features—supervision by the District Court and compulsory conciliation followed by the "option" of arbitration—were consistent with the fundamental principle: centralized supervision of decentralized specialized branches. The original 1895 North Dakota law (as amended in 1913) limited conciliation to cases pending in court in which both parties agreed to the process (Smith, 1924b:17). The first state to adopt a state-wide Small Claims Court act was Massachusetts. The 1920 act was praised for making the "small claims court an integral part of the judicial system" and leaving wide discretion to the courts to adopt and modify rules in an experimental fashion (Willoughby, 1929:315). The act did not create a new court, but required instead that every lower court judge establish special sessions and procedures for hearing all claims under $35. California and South Dakota (1921) and Nevada and Idaho (1923) were among the states that created similar institutions. The North Dakota structure—supervision over small claims proceedings by the District Court judge—was found to be less desirable because the latter did not adequately oversee the conciliation boards.

In contrast to most states, Iowa made conciliation optional with the judge (1923). The American Judicature Society called this a "conservative experiment" (*JAJS*, 1923:15; Harley, 1926), objecting to the exclusion of lawyers and the absence of record. Furthermore, they found that after two years of experimentation there had been "no instance of any judge electing to give the plan a trial" (Harley, 1926:96). Reformers preferred mandatory procedures to increase the use of conciliation and closer supervision in accordance with the principle of unification.

Reformers consistently urged the reduction of litigation through conciliation and called for more compulsion to achieve this goal. They proposed that lower courts adopt rules requiring parties to try conciliation before their dispute would be placed on the court calendar (*JAJS*, 1918c; Lauer, 1928).

Conciliation procedures, such as the Rules on Conciliation of the New York City Municipal Court (1917) were also criticized for failing to ensure the enforceability of agreements. Two separate but related issues were involved in the question of the "legality" of conciliation agreements. First, should parties be required to submit disputes involving certain amounts of money to conciliation; and second, should conciliation agreements be enforceable. On the one hand, Smith criticized "pure conciliation," exemplified by the Kansas Small Debtors' Court, because it was "entirely detached from the regular administration of justice, [and therefore] seems to defeat its own ends" (Smith, 1924a:2). He argued that conciliation tribunals, in contrast with small claims courts, lacked compulsory jurisdiction and the power to enforce agreements and therefore failed to satisfy the goal of providing access to justice for the petty litigant. He recommended, instead, that conciliation procedures be adopted by regular courts and not relegated to "extra-legal" tribunals (Smith, 1924a:3). On the other hand, Smith acknowledged that "compulsion exercised to force a settlement is, of course, not conciliation at all, but unless an agreement can be enforced, the door is left open for fraud by refusal to abide by the adjustment, so that the proceeding merely results in loss of time and disappointment" (Smith, 1919b:64). Smith resolved this conflict by encouraging the use of arbitration to supplement conciliation.

The Kansas Small Debtors' Courts, the Iowa Conciliation Boards, and the New York City conciliation calendar were considered conciliation tribunals rather than Small Claims Courts. Reformers associated such experiments with conciliation in Norway and Denmark, because the tribunals were somewhat independent of the court system and conciliation was optional with either the parties or the judge (Grevstad, 1918;

Smith, 1926). Reformers not only criticized these tribunals because they were unsupervised but also dismissed them as failures. The *New York Law Review* reported in 1925 that the New York City Municipal Court conciliation calendar was a failure because few parties would agree to submit their disputes since the resulting agreements were not enforceable. Willoughby's survey of conciliation tribunals concluded that voluntary conciliation "rarely occur[s] unless careful provision has been made for the establishment of a system of conciliation . . . as an integral feature of the judicial system and this system has received at least legal recognition" (Willoughby, 1929:40). We have little information, however, about who used conciliation and why.

In summary, reformers supported those conciliation experiments that required participation and operated within the context of a unified court system. Both minor criminal and civil disputes were handled by procedures located within existing institutions. Informal procedures complemented conventional adjudication in two respects. First, the flexibility of investigatory proceedings, characteristic of conciliation and arbitration, enabled the judiciary to absorb more conflict (both in kind and intensity), thus appearing to respond to social demands without fundamentally altering existing judicial structures. Second, with the growth of specialization in the lower courts, informal procedures served to channel the exercise of discretion within judicial institutions.

Criticism of the socialized courts after 1940 focuses on the fact that they were appendages of traditional judicial institutions rather than genuine alternatives to the adversarial process. The literature on small claims courts takes the position that informal procedures were nothing more than simplified, streamlined versions of conventional adjudication without due process protection. The "cross-cutting" interests of judges, who sought to expand their role rather than to relinquish jurisdiction to lay conciliators, is often given as the reason (see Yngvesson and Hennessey, 1975). During this early period of reform the concept of due process was not as developed as we understand it today (see Ryerson, 1978:57–58, 63), nor was the distinction between proactive judges and proactive courts as clear. Because they failed to distinguish between courts and judges, delegalization reformers established a complementary adjudication process within what they thought would be a unified court system. But contrary to their desire for a lower court *system* in which specialization would be managed by centralized administration, the socialized courts did not complement a unified lower court but increased the organizational complexity of the judicial structure (Virtue, 1953; Galub, 1968).

Unification continued to be the dominant management strategy. In 1938, the ABA adopted the Parker-Vanderbilt resolution calling for more unified judicial organization through the establishment of administrative judges, judicial councils to make policy, statistical information systems and, once again, the replacement of the justice of the peace courts by municipal courts. Although scientific management techniques used in the industrial sector had by then been influenced by the human development approach (see Baritz, 1960), the legal order was slow to consider the importance of individual behavior for management. Court unification between the 1940s and 1960s was aimed, instead, at greater centralization and control of the judicial work process (Volcansek, 1977).

For the past seventy years, unification has been the predominant goal in reorganizing decentralized trial courts (Gazell, 1977). But attempts to bring lower courts within a unified system have been hindered by local resistance. The county jurisdiction of local courts has presented political and cultural obstacles to a fully rationalized judicial administration (Gallas, 1976).

RECONSTRUCTING JUDICIAL MANAGEMENT WITH INFORMALISM

The quest for a unified judicial system persists despite lessons from the Progressive period and resistance from local courts. The present approach, however, is not simply a rehash of the same old management concepts. Nor do we find the same kinds of informal dispute-processing institutions in both periods. The difference between the small claims court in the

Progressive period and the neighborhood justice center of today is reflected in the differing management strategies of each
period. Whereas scientific management in the Progressive period sought to promote efficient service by *minimizing waste-
ful human motion*, the current judicial management strategy
emphasizes access to justice by *maximizing organizational capacity*. The newer approach is called *decentralized unification*.
It seeks to integrate court-related institutions into the judicial
system. Court-related institutions identified with this approach include: "jails; state prisons; pretrial diversion centers
dealing with such matters as rehabilitation of alcoholics, drug
addicts, and juvenile offenders or delinquents; probation offices; parole boards, prison disciplinary boards; compulsory and
voluntary arbitration panels; conciliation bureaus; pretrial
detention centers; and so-called 'community moots' " (Ashman
and Parness, 1974:40).

Decentralized unification is a broad management strategy.
It expands the scope of administration beyond earlier concerns with managing the *organization* of courts to managing
their organizational *environment*. The fundamental tenets of
court unification are not rejected by the decentralized unification strategy. Instead, they are applied to an array of activity more often associated with social services rather than with
courts. For example, two proponents of this expanded management strategy argue that unification should not be limited
to courts, it should be conceptualized more broadly to encom-
pass court-related institutions thereby building toward a concept of a *unified judicial system* (Ibid.:39). They suggest that
"[c]onsideration of the concept of a unified judicial system would
justify application by the judiciary of the unification principles of centralized supervision to court-related institutions"
(Ibid.:40).

The principal weakness reformers find with the older strategy of court unification is that it over-centralizes courts and
ignores external constraints that impact on courts. The challenge for decentralized unification is to regulate many levels
of the judicial environment. For example, it is argued that less
formal, less rule-bound instruments of management are essential for regulating "uncontrolled resources," such as the

prosecutorial staff, public defender, and probation programs that are part of the local environment (Ibid.:44). Referring to another layer of the judicial environment, one critic of court unification contends that "[w]ithout a large measure of local autonomy, trial-level judges and administrators will be incapable of rapidly adjusting their procedures to respond to changes in their immediate environments" (Hays, 1977:130).

This challenge calls for judicial management of court-related services. Reformers maintain that decentralized organization and management will allow courts the flexibility to incorporate court-related services into a unified judicial system. This strategy seeks to both expand the scope of judicial administration and manage elements indigenous to the local judicial environment.[11]

Since reformers have long recognized that decentralization may lead to over-specialization, why are reformers today supporting a decentralized management strategy? Unlike the specialized branches of the municipal court, court-related institutions do not have exclusive jurisdiction over certain types of cases. One way of curbing over-specialization while retaining a decentralized approach is to develop a referral network that court-related institutions are dependent upon for their cases.[12] Under the decentralized unification strategy, referral networks are on the one hand administrative mechanisms for managing court-related institutions and on the other hand they expand the capacity of the judicial system.

Observers have noted that the "effect [of unification] is likely to depend, in part, upon whether the design is appropriate for the basic production process of the organization and the environment in which it operates" (Henderson and Kerwin, 1982:456). Gallas makes a similar point in a slightly less technical manner: improve the "fit between the technical and social subsystems in the organization" (Gallas, 1976:47). This means that decentralized unification is implemented through the management of different adjudication processes—the production processes of the judicial system. "Each type of adjudicatory process has very different management requirements. The striking fact for an outside observer of courts is how little direct administrative support a judge needs to be effective in procedural adjudication" (Henderson and Kerwin, 1982:457). Henderson and Kerwin emphasize that the need for administrative support increases as the production process becomes more informal.[13]

Decentralized unification is a strategy to respond to diverse forms of decision making without the chaotic proliferation of specialized tribunals, such as those that emerged from the bureaucratic reforms of the Progressive period.[14] The tribunals are specialized (Cappelletti and Garth, 1978), but networks they form link specialized tribunals to produce a unified system. Seen in this light, we can better understand why the second wave of delegalization coincides with the implementation of a decentralized management strategy.

Richard Danzig's proposal (1973) for a decentralized criminal justice system is an example of this management strategy. Danzig described the decentralized "community moot" as a "complementary system, supplementing and in some areas substituting" existing court services (Danzig, 1973:7). The community moot is a court resource that relies heavily upon agents in the criminal justice system for referrals (Ibid.:8). Other community mediation models are even more dependent upon courts (McGillis and Mullen, 1977). Indeed, the first experiments with mediation and arbitration of minor criminal and civil disputes in this period were developed by prosecutors and courts (McGillis, 1980; Florida Supreme Court, 1979). Decentralized court organization thus encourages the evolution of "appended remedy systems" without disrupting the organization of the "official remedy system" (Galanter, 1974) and increases the capacity of the judiciary to create programs—to become proactive.

Another aspect of the judicial "production process" is the work process. Decentralized unification also rationalizes and professionalizes the judicial work process.[15] The use of paraprofessionals (lay mediators) to organize community resources and mediate minor disputes is far more prevalent today than it was during the Progressive era. This has been characterized as "deprofessionalizing" decision making as well. Yet, with a closer examination of the role of paraprofessionals in a decentralized management model, we find that, as Heydebrand describes it, the "fusion of professional-technical and managerial functions into a new set of systemic roles and a new structural synthesis is one of the main characteristics of technocratic administration" (Heydebrand, 1983b:99). Or, in Danzig's words:

A key to successful municipal operation of police, courts, and prisons lies in determining which functions already have been professionalized, which may be feasibly and appropriately professionalized in the near future, and which are not easily or should not be professionalized. The latter are ripe for decentralization. Thus formulated, *decentralization becomes not a force in opposition to professionalization*, but rather a force well coordinated with it, a force which in fact speeds professionalization by shaping the role definition the professional is seeking to assume (Danzig, 1973:9; emphasis added).

Danzig notes that police spend a large percentage of their time performing order maintenance tasks—responding to domestic and neighborhood disturbances—for which "police training and professionalization efforts are least directed," and they exercise discretion in these situations (Ibid.:29). Advocates of pre-trial diversion similarly criticize the mismatch between the training of prosecutors and judges and the type of discretion they must exercise in handling order maintenance problems. In the decentralized model, discretion is exercised within a unified judicial system. As paraprofessionals assume these tasks, a new stratum of court-related personnel are created.[16] The judicial work process then becomes further stratified and rationalized. Efficiency in the delegalization movement means matching different types of disputes with the appropriate technical skills of judicial system personnel.[17] As a result, discretion once exercised by court officials and police officers is formally exercised by mediators and arbitrators in a therapeutic setting. Delegalization in this context serves to rationalize the adjudication process.

The reform objective of efficient service introduced in the Progressive period reemerges in the contemporary delegalization movement, but its application extends beyond a rationale for intervention by courts in order for maintenance to be a justification for intervention by court-related institutions. The shift from centralized judicial management under unification to decentralized management under a unified judicial system necessitates a broader concept of efficient judicial service. Management under decentralization is conducted through networks rather than hierarchical structures. Such an approach has correctly been characterized as the simultaneous centralization and decentralization of courts (Heydebrand, 1979:39–40; Spitzer, 1982). Traditional assumptions about what constitutes judicial activity are on the one hand relaxed by the decentralized unification strategy. Specifically, the distinction between adjudication and administration is blurred for the purposes of redefining what activity is part of the unified judicial system. On the other hand, there is greater stratification between the different production processes within the judicial system. The layers of judicial activity are more clearly differentiated, while the boundaries of the system expand. The simultaneous centralization and decentralization is evidenced in the attention to informal dispute processes and paraprofessionals.

CONCLUSION

The contemporary reform "promises something deeper than technology" (Cover, 1979:912), something more substantive than a mere administrative or technocratic remedy to the problems of access to justice for the powerless. As we discussed in the previous chapter, the Progressives advocated socialized law in socialized courts, and the current delegalization movement seeks to rebuild a legal consensus for judicial intervention through a participatory concept of access to justice. The institutional origins of both ideologies are embedded in the construction and reconstruction of judicial management strategies.

Starting from the premise that courts are limited by their structure (formal procedures) and function (determining innocence or guilt on the basis of legally relevant facts), delegalization reform in both periods is an attempt to expand the judicial capacity of courts and court-related institutions to manage minor disputes through the use of informal procedures, mediation, and arbitration. The objectives of the contemporary delegalization movement are efficient dispute processing and expansion of access to justice in minor criminal and civil disputes. Both goals have antecedents in the Progressive reforms.

Critics of both sets of reforms have argued that these two objectives are in conflict (*The Mooter*, 1977–1980; Singer, 1979). These objectives, however, are *collateral policies* of an administrative-technocratic rationale for judicial intervention in order maintenance. It is apparent that dispute processes premised on a hostility to formality play a significant role in the judicial management strategies of the twentieth century. The expansion of administrative access to justice under such reforms were facilitated by the rise of judicial management and extended through the contemporary decentralization of judicial management. Both objectives were structured by the politics of judicial management—the concentration of judicial power under an ideology of expanding participation.

NOTES

1. Here I am applying Wolf Heydebrand's concept of management strategies developed in his critique of conventional notions of technocracy. He suggests that "the traditional notion of technocracy implies an all-encompassing consciousness and a relatively fixed, one-dimensional system of control. By contrast, it may be more useful and closer to contemporary realities to identify specific technocratic *strategies* that are structurally generated by corporate and governmental decision makers, that are aimed at preventing or dealing with crises and stabilizing the political economy, and that are contradictory in the sense that they embody different forms of rationality and a conflict between short-term and long-term planning" (Heydebrand, 1983b:95).

2. The approach here is not based on organization theory (Feeley, 1973; Eisenstein and Jacob, 1977; Jacob, 1983) or systems theory (Nimmer, 1978); nor am I viewing courts as bureaucracies (Blumberg, 1967). Rather I am interested in examining management strategies applied to lower courts. We can identify the mode of rationalization associated with management strategies by studying two related court processes: the organization of court personnel (the judicial work process) and procedures for processing disputes (the adjudication

process). I am interested in the institutional origins of delegalization ideology. This approach does not explain the rise of particular forms of judicial management. Richard Hofrichter (1982) has attempted to link legal changes to economic and political constraints on the state; see also Hirschhorn (1978) and O'Connor (1973: Chs. 2, 5, 6).

3. Many statutes required annual audits of the justice of the peace courts. This was one way of supervising these courts, however, rarely were audits done (Silverstein, 1955:245).

4. In 1866 the Boston Municipal Court was established to assume the jurisdiction of the JP courts (civil) and the Boston Police Court (criminal). A municipal court was established in New York City in 1898. These were both considered "old" municipal courts because they lacked an administrative structure (see Roesch, 1904; Greene, 1910).

5. B. E. Sunny, president of the Chicago Telephone Company, and Bernard Eckhart, described by Harley as a "wealthy miller and grain dealer" (Harley, 1917b:4; see also Gilbert, 1928; Kogan, 1974; Chapter 1).

6. See Ryerson (1978) for a discussion of the relationship between the creation of a new stratum of court officials and developments occurring within the social sciences. (Also see Rothman, 1980: Chapter 3).

7. This philosophy advocated "decriminalization" of domestic relations disputes. Reformers argued that defendants should not be treated like criminals. The use of a summons instead of an arrest was seen as a step toward "decriminalizing" these disputes. One study found that 90 percent of those summoned appeared in court "voluntarily" (Zunser, 1926). The summons, however, was backed by the coercive power of a bench warrant if the defendant did not show up. It appears that "decriminalization" represented little more than the use of less overtly coercive incentives to ensure compliance.

8. The actors in this reform movement were a highly unified group, made up of trade associations of lawyers and judges, such as the American Judicature Society. Although there was considerable unity of opinion (Yngvesson and Hennessey, 1975:225), reformers did disagree about particular types of informal tribunals.

9. The first experiment with conciliation that reformers discuss in any detail occurred in the policy prosecutor's office in Cleveland in 1904. Under the Municipal Court Act, parties in minor criminal cases who were unable to pay for counsel would meet with the deputy clerk, selected by the municipal judge, and he would assist them in reaching an out-of-court settlement (Levine, 1915).

10. It is interesting to note that the American Bar Association, the Association of Credit Men, the Chamber of Commerce, and the other influential advocates of small claims courts did not support religious tribunals such as the Baltimore Jewish Court of Arbitration. Three lay persons presided over this tribunal in which lawyers were not allowed to participate and the parties had to agree to arbitration (see Hartogensis, 1929).

11. One example of integrating resources from the environment into the court is the Community Resource Program, which is "designed to more fully utilize community resources and probation services by the court, and to provide the court [with] mechanisms to develop resources previously unavailable" (American Judicature Society and Institute for Court Management, 1978:46–47).

12. Eric Fisher's "community court" (1975) is an exception, it proposes that minor dispute resolution programs have statutory jurisdiction. This model has not been adopted yet, but the movement towards establishing and institutionalizing alternatives may apply Fisher's basic concept.

13. Henderson and Kerwin (1982) distinguish levels of administrative assistance across three adjudicatory processes. Procedural adjudication requires the lowest level of administrative support. Decisional (e.g., denial of bail) and diagnostic (e.g., family and domestic relations) adjudication processes demand more administrative assistance.

14. Heydebrand argues that Weber's concept of bureaucracy is not applicable to many modern rationalized organizations and that it has been misapplied to what he called "technocratic administration" (Heydebrand, 1983a). Technocratic administration is a new form of organization and control differing from the Weberian concept of bureaucracy in important ways. The distinctions Heydebrand makes between these two modes of organization and administration may in fact describe organizational and administrative differences between the bureaucratic model in Progressive reforms (e.g., hierarchical authority and routinizable) and the technocratic approach of contemporary reforms (e.g., decentralized and non-routine with "inter-organizational networks").

15. Another indicator that the alternative dispute resolution field is being professionalized is the American Bar Association and program mediators' growing interest in developing professional ethics for mediation. The organization most concerned with this issue is the Society for Professionals in Dispute Resolution, an organization affiliated with the American Arbitration Association. Another step to-

ward professionalization is certification, which the legal profession has been focusing some attention on recently. Although a proposal submitted to the Family Law Section of the ABA requiring that mediators be certified lawyers did not pass, there is an active campaign to introduce alternative dispute resolution materials into law school curriculum. See the following essays for an overview of alternative dispute resolution in the law school curriculum: Sander (1984); and Sacks (1984).

16. Ronald Pipkin and Janet Rifkin (1984) found in their study of the social backgrounds of mediation program employees that the administrators tend to be older men making higher salaries, while the program staff and mediators are largely younger women, marginally employed or working as volunteers. All three groups (administrators, staff, and mediators), however, had similar educational backgrounds. It is not surprising that highly educated yet marginally employed service workers are attempting to professionalize their practice. It is not clear at this point how successful they will be.

17. Although initially some effort was made by the U.S. Justice Department to promote NJCs as cost effective programs (see Law Enforcement Assistance Administration, 1979:1), notions of efficiency are not limited to simple cost accounting. Prevention and rehabilitation have been suggested as two "alternative" criteria for measuring the efficiency of NJCs. This shift in judicial management strategies resembles the reorganization and rationalization of social services (see Hirschhorn, 1978:68).

CHAPTER THREE

The Politics of Legal Resources

Making public policy on alternative dispute resolution involves a political struggle about the definition and distribution of legal resources. Not since the creation of the federally funded Office of Economic Opportunity (OEO) Legal Service Program in 1968, or the advent of privately funded public interest law firms in 1970, has there been as much discussion about the delivery and distribution of legal resources as we witness with the alternatives movement. By the late 1970s congressional hearings began to address once again the allocation of legal resources and "access to justice." In reviewing those hearings, one is struck by the range of political groups pushing for a national dispute resolution program. Despite the ideological diversity among those advocating mediation, a national coalition did form to pass the Dispute Resolution Act (1980). How was this policy fashioned; what are the political struggles leading to its formation?

The rights theme, consistent throughout earlier debates over legal resources, dropped out of the policy discussion on alternative dispute resolution. When the political struggle for legal resources focused on problems of the poor and the underrepresented, rights were taken seriously. In the alternatives movement *legal resources are not rights, they are institutions to fa-*

cilitate negotiation and mediation. The principal concern is with
preserving the institutional capacity of courts and of disputants to reach settlements rather than protect rights. Does this
shift represent a politics of retreat? Retreat, that is, from the
politics of rights (Scheingold, 1974). And if so, what accounts
for the political diversity within the alternatives movement and
the coalition to establish a national policy on dispute resolution?

From a broader historic perspective, this struggle is framed
within the boundaries of a reconstructed judicial management
strategy. That is, underlying the debates and strategic decisions on alternative dispute resolution policy is a framework
for organizing institutional practices, a framework that cen-
tralizes and decentralizes authority over legal resources. We
have traced the development of judicial management, both its
ideology and institutional setting. Now we turn to the political arena of policy formation. This chapter first examines legislative debates on distributing resources for dispute processing. It discusses the political dynamics of the struggle for power
and control over legal resources. We then examine how the
political struggles over legal resources are connected to experiments in mediating social conflict.

DEFINING RESOURCES

Old alliances were broken and new ones were forged in the
process of defining the nature and distribution of legal resources. Traditional boundaries, such as those separating
criminal and civil disputes, broke down as did the governmental agencies assigned to maintain them. For example, the
community crime prevention concerns of the Law Enforcement Assistance Administration (LEAA) overlapped with civil
justice dispute resolution such that LEAA began funding programs outside what had been traditionally defined as the
criminal justice system. Indeed, it was LEAA who funded many
of the early dispute programs (1971–1975),[1] including programs in prosecutors' offices (The Columbus Night Prosecutor
Program, 1971); lower criminal courts (Boston Urban Court
Project, 1975); state court programs (Miami Dispute Settle-

ment Program, 1975); and privately sponsored programs (IMCR-Manhattan and Bronx Dispute Resolution Centers, 1975).[2] What new political alliance made up the access to justice movement, and under what conditions did it form?

Just as the American Bar Association (ABA) has been a principal actor in a variety of judicial reforms, including those in the Progressive period, it has played a leadership role in the formation of national policy on alternatives. This is not to suggest that the ABA substituted the cause of alternatives for its campaign on legal services, however, the ABA's leadership role in this area is not without impact when it came to setting priorities and shaping national policy. The ABA Conference on Popular Dissatisfaction with the Administration of Justice (1976) launched a national campaign to experiment with mediation and arbitration. Following the recommendations of this conference (the Pound Conference), the U.S. Department of Justice created the Office for Improvements in the Administration of Justice (OIAJ) (Judicial Conference of the ABA, 1976; Sanders, 1977). One of OIAJ's main responsibilities was to promote national attention and provide leadership for the development of informal minor dispute processes.

In partnership with the Carter Justice Department, the ABA furnished guidelines for the neighborhood justice concept. Griffin Bell, soon to be appointed Attorney General by President Carter, spoke at the Pound Conference on behalf of the neighborhood justice concept. Shortly after the conference, the ABA established the Special Committee on Resolution of Minor Disputes. The ABA emphasized that the forum should "fit the fuss" (Rosenberg, 1976), thereby reducing overcrowded court conditions and providing disputants with a faster, cheaper, and more specialized forum for resolving disputes than court. The ABA Committee believed that alternative mechanisms would eliminate the need for judicial action and therefore be a cost-saving device (Dellapa, 1977). Early dispute programs such as the Citizen Dispute Settlement Program in Orlando, Florida were funded by the Bar (see Conner and Surette, 1977).

The National Institute of Law Enforcement and Criminal Justice (NILECJ), in conjunction with OIAJ developed three experimental pilot neighborhood justice centers in 1978: Atlanta, court sponsored; Los Angeles, Bar sponsored; and Kansas City, Missouri, city government sponsored. These neighborhood justice centers were established with the cooperation of local sponsors, but were required to follow the national guidelines. The NILECJ guidelines called for the creation of mediation programs to resolve minor criminal and civil disputes. The program objectives that were incorporated in the guidelines included: the reduction of court case load by diverting disputes to mediation that were inappropriate for an adversarial process; the development of fair and lasting solutions for everyday minor conflicts; and the establishment of a referral and information service for disputes that can be handled outside court (see Cook et al., 1980:8).

The American Friends Service Committee (AFSC), a private nonprofit Quaker organization, was also active in developing alternatives in the 1970s. In 1972, AFSC established the Pre-trial Justice Program, which provided pre-trial diversion mediation services. As a result of this experience with pre-trial services, the AFSC became a national advocate for grass roots programs. Grass roots dispute programs are informal dispute programs developed by community groups and independent of the prosecutor's office or courts (Wahrhaftig, 1978; *The Mooter*, 1977–1980). Although not an AFSC project, AFSC designated the San Francisco Community Board Program, established in 1978, as a model for other grass roots projects.[3] It continues to serve as the non–court-based community model.

Private organizations sought to mobilize the fragmented and unorganized dispute resolution programs into a national movement beginning in 1979 with the Cherry Hill Conference. This conference, sponsored by the New Jersey Office of the Public Advocate's Dispute Resolution Program, served as an initial effort to train, lobby for the Dispute Resolution Act, and network among developing and established informal dispute programs.[4]

The political orientations of those supporting alternatives ranged from the conservatism of Chief Justice Burger to the liberalism of the AFSC. And the congressional hearings in the late 1970s on legal resources and access to justice served as an important arena for these diverse political orientations to struggle over the definition and distribution of legal resources. Representatives from business, consumer groups, the legal profession, academia, private foundations, and the judiciary appeared before several different committees to express their interests in minor dispute processing. While in some instances there was direct opposition by consumer advocates to Chamber of Commerce proposals, tentative alliances between other groups were established along the way. In the end, a policy on legal resources for minor dispute resolution was established. Funding for a national program has yet to be secured, however, the policy remains intact.[5] The policy was shaped around two political struggles: (1) what type of resources for what disputes, and (2) what role the federal government will have in administering the program.

From Rights to Institutions

In his final report on the Dispute Resolution Act of 1980, Representative Robert Kastenmeier (D-WI), chairman of the House Judiciary Subcommittee on Courts, Civil Liberties, and the Administration of Justice, identified three legislative goals in the access to justice debates from 1977 to 1980. He said:

The federal government is not interested in silencing a particular barking dog or solving a given family squabble; it is interested in assuring that forums exist at the State and local level to resolve these disputes so that State and local governments may *preserve public order, promote harmony* among citizens and *guarantee access to equal justice* (Kastenmeier, 1979:15; emphasis added).

Two years earlier, in 1977, these same three goals were advanced in the oversight hearings on the "State of the Judiciary and Access to Justice" (U.S. H.R. Judiciary Committee, 1977). At those hearings, Chief Justice Burger submitted written testimony concurring with Attorney General Bell's position that these goals could best be met by developing "the counterpart" to the old justice of the peace courts—neighborhood justice centers. "The concept of neighborhood justice centers," Bell said, "is not to use coercion. If you had to have the coercive power of the court, people would be sent to the court house. The ideal way would be to run these neighborhood offices as branches of the court clerk's office, and all of these things would be done by persuasion" (Bell, 1977:72).

Ralph Nader's Public Citizen Litigation Group, was reluctant to reverse the course of a decade-long struggle to expand legal advocacy. Although they did support some aspects of the neighborhood justice concept,[6] they were also cautious about going along with the Justice Department-ABA coalition. The Director of the Legal Service Corporation, Thomas Ehrlich, was equally reluctant to join this coalition. Ehrlich warned that there "is a danger, which we have seen, that the new forums will become institutionalized screening mechanisms for moving cases out of the court system instead of attempts to deliver justice with better results and greater access by the public" (Ehrlich, 1977:47). Consumer and public interest groups shared this concern: access to *equal* justice may conflict with the other two goals of promoting harmony and maintaining public order and result in shutting court doors to underrepresented groups.

The legislative battle over defining legal resources and access to equal justice did not begin, however, in 1977 with the House oversight hearings. It had been going on at least since 1973 when consumer groups fought hard for a national consumer protection agency, a battle that was eventually lost. The congressional hearings on minor disputes in the late 1970s provided yet another opportunity for consumer advocates to press for national assistance. They did so in 1977 by supporting the Consumer Controversies Resolution (H.R. 2482), a bill to establish a consumer-oriented dispute program. It would have created an Office of Consumer Redress in the Federal Trade Commission (FTC). The Office of Consumer Redress was to function as a national resource center; collect information on existing consumer complaint mechanisms; coordinate state planning with national goals; and make funds available for demonstration projects. A similar bill (H.R. 2965), also introduced in the Commerce Committee, proposed that the Secretary of Commerce establish and operate the resource center instead of the FTC. Mark Green, director of the Public Citizen's Congress Watch, noted that both bills had provisions for substantially less funding (25 million dollars) compared to 1973 consumer legislation (95 million dollars) (Green, 1978:76).

While these hearings in the Commerce Committee were going on, the Senate and House judiciary committees began drafting what would later become the Dispute Resolution Act of 1980 (S. 957, 1978 and H.R. 2863, 1979). These bills called for the establishment of informal mechanisms to handle a *range* of minor criminal and civil disputes, not only consumer problems. In fact, during the legislative hearings, more attention was given to neighborhood disputes than consumer problems. Many consumer groups strongly opposed the committees' inclination to merge national resources for consumer problems with a program on minor criminal disputes (e.g., Public Citizen's Congress Watch, Consumer Protection Center, New York City Bar Consumer Affairs Commission, the National Association of Consumer Agency Administration, the National Consumer League, and the Consumer Union).

Consumer groups challenged this proposal in an effort both to advance consumer rights and, perhaps more immediately, preserve some type of national commitment to consumer protection. Critics argued that unlike neighborhood disputes consumer problems had "clear-cut legal precedents" and that these rights were essential for redressing the "imbalance in the marketplace between purchaser of a product and the seller" (Green, 1978:76). They believed that the Dispute Resolution bill was trying to do too much with too few resources. A program that combines the "barking dog and the broken toasters" will ultimately be ineffective in increasing access to justice for either kind of dispute (Ibid.:77). Consumer advocates pointed to the well known danger in many small claims reform measures, like this one, of creating collection agencies for business. Specifically, they objected to S. 957, which resembled the Chamber of Commerce's Model Small Claims Court Act (see U.S. Judiciary Committee, 1978:437), because no limits were placed on the use of the dispute mechanism by small businesses, corporations, partnerships and assignees (see S. 957, section 4(a)(5)(D)). And finally, consumer groups criticized both bills and the Chamber of Commerce's Model Small

Claims proposal for prohibiting the use of funds for paying attorneys' fees (see S. 957 section 7 (d) (2)).

President Carter's Office of Consumer Affairs supported the
Dispute Resolution Act (S. 957). The acting director said that
efforts "must be taken to insure noneconomic disputes do not
dominate the activities of the funded mechanisms under the
program," yet he maintained that the Dispute Resolution Act
incorporated this concern (Richardson, 1978:89). The Department of Justice's Office for Improvements in the Administration of Justice more clearly did not want to pass a "pure" consumer bill. They joined with the American Bar Association, the
Chamber of Commerce, the Better Business Bureau, the
American Arbitration Association, and the National Home
Improvement Association to defeat both Commerce Committee bills (H.R. 2482 and H.R. 2965), and to support the neighborhood justice program.

The organized opposition to consumer advocacy pushed for
delegalizing the treatment of minor disputes. Assistant Attorney General Daniel Meador, the director of OIAJ, said the
"process in a justice center is not the same as in the court.
The dispute is not necessarily resolved in accordance with any
legal rules. It may be worked out in a practical common sense
way between the parties. Indeed the very idea is to have a kind
of nonlegalized process. You know we are overlegalized in this
country, too many regulations, too many laws and so on"
(Meador, 1978:76). Delegalization, they believed, would revi-
talize informal dispute functions that had been performed by
traditional social institutions, such as the family, schools,
churches, and local police. The neighborhood justice concept
was, from this perspective, an effort to establish private informal dispute-processing institutions (see Sarat and Grossman,
1975) in a public informal setting.

Community organizers who appeared at the legislative
hearings supported this position as well. The director of the
San Francisco Community Board Program, Raymond Shonholtz, responded to consumer activists by emphasizing a different set of concerns than those of the public interest law
movement. Shonholtz argued that the critical issues facing
urban America stemmed from *unresolved* conflicts, not simply

unrepresented disputes (Shonholtz, 1978:133–138). This distinction between resolving disputes and representing the unrepresented is what separated the consumer advocates from the community organizers in these legislative debates.

Business groups found the neighborhood justice emphasis on building consensus between parties through private negotiations very attractive. The National Home Improvement Council endorsed the Dispute Resolution Act, as did J.C. Penney Co., Sears, the Motor Vehicle Manufacturers Association, the National Manufactured Housing Federation, and the Ohio Mobile Home and Recreational Vehicle Association. The Chamber of Commerce applauded the bill because in their view it was a "bill which transcends ideological lines and enjoys a unique coalition of the administration, consumer and business groups, as well as that of lawyers' groups and representatives of State and local governments. . . . S. 957, in facilitating the establishment and improvement of informal dispute resolution mechanisms and Small Claims Courts, with its *careful restraints on government intervention* and its reasonable price tag, ultimately may be the solution to providing effective redress for consumer problems" (Schultz, 1978:133; emphasis added).

The ABA was of course very enthusiastic about the neighborhood justice concept. The voluntary nature of the proposed dispute mechanisms were hailed by the legal profession as essential for the protection of legal rights and the functioning of a private informal process.

Administration of Alternative Dispute Resolution Resources

The role of the federal government in administering the program was the second controversial issue. What government agency should administer the program, and how much authority should that agency have in determining the kind of neighborhood justice centers to be developed? These questions are central to federalism, the relationship between federal and state governments, and ultimately the role of community participation in the neighborhood justice movement.

The first dispute-processing bills introduced in the House Commerce Committee placed the administrative responsibility in the FTC and Commerce Department. Once the Senate and House Judiciary Committees introduced their minor dispute bills, the Department of Justice began bidding for the job. Other federal agencies, such as the Legal Services Corporation (LSC) and LEAA, were considered as candidates for the job, but were firmly rejected. The Department of Justice opposed placing administrative functions in the LSC, arguing that the LSC lacked the resources to do research on non-judicial mechanisms (Meador, 1978:66). The LSC agreed, but for different reasons. Ehrlich suggested that such "a scheme might undercut the credibility and objectivity of the Corporation as well as the objectives of the Act" (Ehrlich, 1978:129). LEAA was unanimously rejected because its own future was in question and it had been established to deal with criminal matters only, despite its early involvement in the dispute resolution field.

The ABA and the Chamber of Commerce joined the OIAJ, an arm of the Department of Justice, in supporting a proposal that placed the national clearinghouse and authority to make grants for Neighborhood Justice Centers in the Department of Justice. They argued that the Department of Justice had been involved in a wide range of both civil and criminal matters and even though the program was not a state court program, it would be the most efficient agency for channeling funds to state programs or independent projects. The ABA Special Committee on Resolution of Minor Disputes urged that the Department of Justice be chosen because it had the resources to centralize technical information on the research and development of alternatives (D'Alemberte and Johnson, 1979). In endorsing the bill (S. 957), which located the administration of dispute resolution resources in the Department of Justice, the National Home Improvement Council commented that by "shifting the oversight process from the Federal Trade Commission to the Justice Department, much private sector criticism has been averted" (Seifert, 1978:265). Assurances that the program would *not* bolster consumer rights were apparently implicit in the proposal for its administration by the Department of Justice.

Consumer advocates wanted the FTC to administer dispute resolution resources. During the second round of legislation in 1979, when it was clear that the proposal for a consumer-oriented program had lost to the neighborhood justice program, they dropped their earlier argument about expertise and suggested instead that state and local diversity would more likely flourish in the FTC. The proposed FTC administrative structure provided that the FTC would function, along with the Attorney General, as a consultant to state and local groups, leaving more discretion in their hands. Consumers Union, Public Citizen's Congress Watch, and the National Association of Consumer Agency Administration opposed the alternative that would centralize administrative powers in the Department of Justice. They feared that states with more progressive consumer laws would then be required to comply with federal guidelines, such as those permitting business to initiate the dispute mechanisms. New York, for example, does not allow credit agencies to use Small Claims Court (Green, 1978).

Groups seeking to protect state and local autonomy and promote diversity in dispute programs were sympathetic to the criticisms offered by consumer advocates on this point. The Conference of State Chief Justices, for example, proposed that a national board, similar to the LSC, administer the program. This board would be independent of the executive department and would not have authority over decisions regarding state court funding.

The community organizers who had joined the Justice Department coalition to back the neighborhood justice program over a consumer program were even more opposed to placing administrative powers in the Department of Justice. The American Friends Service Committee proposed instead that an independent board, comprised of an equal mix of representatives from government, non-government, and community groups, be delegated the administrative responsibility under the Dispute Resolution Act. AFSC's concern was that grass roots programs would be at a disadvantage if the power to administer the program was in the Department of Justice. AFSC felt that community participation would play a larger role in grant decisions if non-government–non-profit groups and community groups were represented on the governing board. Shonholtz opposed the Department of Justice proposal for these same reasons. He argued that groups who were sensitive to neighborhood problems would be more appropriate for this role. Specifically, he suggested that either the LSC expand its mission into this area, or community programs under Housing and Urban Development (HUD), Action, or Health, Education and Welfare (HEW) be given the administrative powers.

Consumer, community, and state judicial opposition to delegating administrative powers to the Department of Justice failed. The heterogenous coalition that formed to create a neighborhood-oriented informal dispute program broke down over who should administer the program. Grass roots advocates, such as AFSC and the San Francisco Community Board Program, lost on an issue central to the politics of the neighborhood justice concept: who should have the power to administer alternative dispute mechanisms? These groups feared that the Department of Justice would be more favorable to court-related alternatives, such as prosecutor referral programs, and thus informal dispute mechanisms would be institutionalized rather than based in the community. Ehrlich's earlier warning about the dangers of institutionalizing "screening mechanisms" became the issue grass roots advocates would lose once they joined the coalition of government, business, and legal professionals to construct a neighborhood-oriented program.

The Dispute Resolution Act unanimously passed both Houses in 1980. The Act defines informal dispute mechanisms as: "courts of limited jurisdiction and arbitration, mediation, conciliation, and similar procedures, and referral services, which are available to adjudicate, settle, and resolve disputes involving small amounts of money or otherwise arising in the course of daily life." It mandates the creation of a Dispute Resolution Resource Center within the Department of Justice. This clearinghouse was established in 1983. The only federal funding to result from the Act has been the National Dispute Resolution Resource Center, despite Chief Justice Warren Burger's repeated call for a "comprehensive review of the whole subject of alternatives to courts" (Ad Hoc Panel on Dispute Resolution, 1983:1), bipartisan support from both Republican and

Democratic U.S. Attorney Generals since 1978, and continuing support from the ABA. Seventeen states, however, have passed dispute resolution legislation since 1980 (Freedman, 1984).

The legislative activity culminating in the passage of the Dispute Resolution Act defined legal resources as facilities for private negotiations. Apart from challenges to this definition by public interest consumer groups, a political coalition of the legal profession, the state, business, and community organizers formed. Within that coalition factions, such as the community organizers, contested *the form* of a decentralized unified judicial system rather than *the content* itself. How centralized should a federally funded program on dispute resolution be if it were to draw on local resources?

Legislative proposals continue to address this issue. The State Institute for Justice Act of 1983 is an example of the Conference of Chief Justices and the Conference of State Court Administrators' effort to create an intermediate institution. The proposed institution interfaces the federal and state judicial systems. It will have responsibility over allocating federal money to a variety of state programs, including alternative dispute resolution (see Freedman, 1984).

At yet another level, policy formation for a decentralized unified judicial system continues on the matter of institutionalizing alternative dispute processing. The policy of institutionalizing alternatives has been underway since the first experiments with neighborhood justice centers (see Chapters 2 and 4). The model of a court with multiple programs and dispute-processing options is not a recent proposal (Sanders, 1977; Cratsley, 1978; Galanter, 1981). The most recent experiment launched by the American Bar Association with support from the Department of Justice (Multi-Door Dispute Resolution Center), however, is explicitly presented as an experiment in institutionalization (*Dispute Resolution*, Winter 1984). Central administration is essential to institutionalization in a decentralized judicial system (see Chapter 2). The Ad Hoc Panel on Dispute Resolution, co-sponsored by the Department of Justice and the National Institute for Dispute Resolution, calls for a "centralized system to be established to screen complaints and refer them to the appropriate dispute resolution mechanism" (Ad Hoc Panel on Dispute Resolution and Public Policy, 1983:23).

MEDIATING CONFLICT

The national policy debate on informalism has placed more attention on minor criminal and civil disputes than mediation of public policy issues or international relations. It is, however, important to locate minor criminal and civil disputes within the larger arena of mediation experiments. Figure 1 identifies some of the major categories of disputes, ranging from individuals vs. individuals to organizations vs. organizations, and the subject areas they address. These disputes have been targeted for alternative dispute resolution mainly because all have been linked to a central theme in the movements: informal dispute resolution works best for parties in ongoing or continuous relationships. The extent and nature of these continuing relationships include intimate family situations as well as nations engaged in long-term policymaking. Mediation and negotiation techniques are also being applied to public policy issues, such as environmental disputes (Amy, 1983; Susskind and Ozawa, 1983).

Different dispute resolution models have been incorporated into the alternatives movement (e.g., community based, court based, institutional grievance mechanisms, administrative procedures, and independent services). Figure 1 shows the kind of dispute resolution model most often associated with particular types of disputes.[7] In the next chapter some of those models will be examined more closely. The purpose here is to situate minor criminal and civil disputes within the range of alternative dispute resolution activity.

In addition to locating minor criminal and civil dispute resolution along a continuum of program models, we need to look at the socio-legal context of the neighborhood justice program. Prior to the development of a national policy on neighborhood justice, mediation had been applied to community disputes involving claims of racial discrimination, institutional grievances, and consumer and family disputes. In these settings,

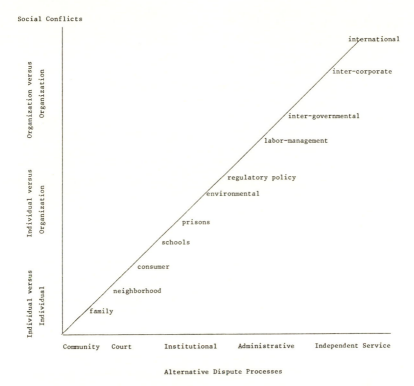

Figure 1.   Disputes and Alternative Dispute Resolution Models

labor-management techniques are substituted for statutory and constitutional law standards. The shift from rights to institutions, which we see emerging from congressional debates over legal resources, has its roots in a shift from rights to preserving relationships. Thus, another dimension of the political struggle over legal resources is the preservation rather than the transformation of social relationships.

Consensus Building in Mediating Community Relations

In response to the racial unrest and the intensification of urban disorder in the 1960s, the federal government created the Community Relations Service under the authority of the 1964 Civil Rights Act, Title X. The purpose of the Community Relations Service was to "organize local advisory panels of citizens in some forty localities to alert the agency to potentially serious disputes and to intervene in conflicts involving public housing, economic development, education, and police conduct" (Ford Foundation, 1978:4). Disputes between ethnic groups over the control of community programs, such as the anti-poverty programs, and conflicts over the administration of government contracts and the regulation of housing authorities are the kinds of conflicts the Community Relations Service was established to mediate. The courts are authorized to refer cases in which they believe that voluntary compliance with the Civil Rights Act can best be achieved through mediation.

Following this effort by the federal government, a number of privately funded community mediation programs were established. In 1968 the Ford Foundation began funding local advisory panels to develop alert systems at the local level and establish mediation services. Similar to the federal government's program, these panels were concerned with mediating racial disputes before they escalated into highly explosive situations. The Ford Foundation funded mediation and arbitration programs, such as the National Center for Dispute Settlement (1968), sponsored by the American Arbitration Association (AAA). The Center later became known as the Community Dispute Service. The principal tasks of the Community Dispute Service were to train community mediators and arbitrators and mediate community conflicts. In 1970 the Institute for Mediation and Conflict Resolution (IMCR) was established with Ford Foundation support. IMCR also trained community interveners, though it placed greater emphasis on mediation than on arbitration.

Labor-management techniques are central in the training programs and philosophy of both IMCR and AAA. The main similarity between labor conflicts and community conflicts is what Fuller calls the "bilateral monopoly" of certain community relationships (Fuller, 1971:310). A "bilateral monopoly" is a situation in which community groups are dependent on one another and have little choice but to seek peaceful resolution of their conflicts. From this assertion of group dependency it is deduced that community groups are under pressure to negotiate: *dependent relationships create incentives to negotiate.* These incentives are more social in nature than labor-management bargaining incentives, which most often are economically based. However, IMCR argued that the exchange model of collective bargaining applies as well to community dispute bargaining, because there is a need to maintain the relationship. The pressures within a continuing dependent relationship, IMCR and AAA argued, put both parties in the position of exchanging or compromising to preserve the relationship itself (Nicolau and Cormick, 1972; Stulberg, 1975). Finally, community mediation advocates apply the contract model used in labor-management to implement and enforce mediated agreements. Contracts provide guidelines for future community interactions as well.

Challenges to the use of labor-management mediation techniques in the area of community conflict came from those who believed that statutory provisions in the 1964, 1965, and 1968 Civil Rights Acts should be the principal guidelines for resolving community disputes involving racial conflict (Blumrosen, 1972). These statutes established *rules* for decision making, while labor-management does not. To introduce labor-management mediation in this area, Alfred Blumrosen argued, was to undermine the efforts of the civil rights movement to mobilize legal resources for their political battles and erode the legal protections against racial discrimination and the remedies for those discriminated against.

Advocates of community mediation responded by contending that labor-management disputes and community disputes are similar in that the law in both areas is not settled on issues of resource allocation. According to the former director of IMCR, George Nicolau, "community disputes go far beyond [the] rather narrow area of statutory standards and their claimed violation" (Nicolau and Cormick, 1972:101). Nicolau and Cormick believe that "the real distinction is not, as Professor Blumrosen maintains, between labor-management disputes and community disputes, but between disputes that are determinable through a body of law and those which are not" (Ibid.:100–

101). Community disputes raise resource allocation issues such as the distribution of resources in federally funded programs, not anticipated nor predetermined by civil rights statutes.[8] Instead of resorting to statutes for guidelines to allocation questions, IMCR argued that in social conflicts "the first guidepost is the bargaining process itself" (Ibid.:102).

Moreover, IMCR argued that to settle community disputes and prevent them from erupting into urban riots or gang violence, the parties should be actively involved in the dispute process. The key to community dispute resolution, they suggest, is an open negotiation process that helps bring underlying issues to the surface. This formula requiries shifting away from legal definitions of disputable issues and turning to the parties themselves for a definition of the dispute. To do so would engage the parties more directly in negotiating a settlement. IMCR maintained that the agreements produced by such negotiations would be long lasting; community mediation was thus seen as a preventative measure (Ford Foundation, 1978).

Mediation of racial disputes, therefore, is not only viewed as a tool for resolving unsettled law, but proponents claim it can be part of a long-term consensus-building process. IMCR suggests that the adjudication process, in contrast to mediation, tends to spark hostility between the parties because it closes off communication that is not directly relevant to the legal issues in question. A consensus-building process, they argued, must first allow conflict to surface. Advocates of community mediation are of course relying on there being an overriding interest in preserving community relationships for mediation to work. Like supporters of labor-management mediation (see Simkin, 1971), community mediation favors a process that makes conflict visible, while containing it in an informal private negotiation process.[9] In both settings mediation relies on an interest in preserving social relations.

The Withering Away of Due Process Protections to Preserve Enduring Client Relationships

Charles Reich's description of social relations in the welfare state (see Reich, 1964; 1965; 1966) is quite similar to the conditions of community life as described by IMCR and AAA. However, where dependency, mutual incentives, and agreement establish the bases for mediating racial disputes, these conditions are offered as reasons for expanding due process protections in Reich's analysis of institutional grievances. Similar descriptions of social relations do not always produce agreement over what should be done. This seems to be the case not only where two slightly different social settings are compared (racial disputes and institutional grievances). It is also true when informal institutional grievance reforms are compared with Reich's view of the welfare state. Both share the same description of social relations inside welfare state institutions, but reach different conclusions about the role of rights in "mediating" conflict.

The scope of due process protections for recipients of state benefits, Reich argued, should not be determined by the old rights/privilege distinction (*Bailey v. Richardson* 341 U.S. 918, 1951; see Van Alstyne, 1968). Instead of a privilege, state benefits are entitlements requiring some due process guarantees. Reich maintained that because of the expansion of state services, "people came to rely on the public largess and framed their expectations and conduct in accord with perceived criteria by which the government distributed needed goods and opportunites" (*Harvard Law Review*, 1976:90). Statutory entitlements not only created *expectations*, they also contributed to a growing *dependency* on state services.

Together, new expectations created by the welfare state and dependency on state benefits produced what Reich called "new property" and new liberty interests. The denial of state benefits without due process would deprive "citizens of the wealth and opportunities they required for the enjoyment of life" (Ibid.:91). Due process protection should also be extended, Reich argued, to control the abuse of bureaucratic discretion. Checks on bureaucratic decision making, he belieived, would enhance access to justice in public institutions by establishing more uniform criteria for the allocation of benefits.

This perspective summarizes the strategy law reformers adopted during the late 1960s and early 1970s. Its impact was felt when the U.S. Supreme Court incorporated portions of Reich's argument in the first entitlement case of that decade,

Goldberg v. Kelly (397 U.S. 254, 1970). Due process protections were extended to other institutions as well. Daily decisions involving the treatment of juveniles, prisoners, students, and government employees were simply no longer considered bureaucratic prerogatives.[10]

Shortly after the U.S. Supreme Court's decision to extend rudimentary due process protections to students threatened with suspension, *Goss v. Lopez* (419 U.S. 566, 1975), a *counter due process movement* emerged (Glazer, 1975; Barton, 1975; Goldstein, 1976; Wilkinson, 1976; Verkuil, 1976; Kirp, 1976). Although conservatives sharply criticized the extension of due process protections, negative reactions to "Goss-like" solutions for institutional grievances did not only come from conservative corners. Indeed, to fully understand the politics of this movement it is important to identify and distinguish its various parts. Its political diversity encompassed defenders of bureaucratic discretion, who were more often than not conservative in their politics, and the left-liberals who drew attention to the limits of procedural rights. These two forces played a major role in moving away from due process and toward experimentation with informal grievance procedures.

For those who saw due process as a threat to bureaucratic authority, emphasis was placed on the need to preserve enduring client relationships. "The key issue that must be faced with respect to this expansion of procedural requirements," Goldstein said, "is how it can be accomplished without destroying the fundamental institutional relationship that the procedures are designed to protect" (Goldstein, 1976:675). These critics appropriated Reich's logic, but argued instead that the *incentives against confrontation* with institutional authorities are especially strong in dependent relationships. Barton and others suggested that from a cost-benefit perspective the choice to exercise due process rights has substantial costs (e.g., reprisals against the client, diversion of funds to pay for due process procedure) for people who are ultimately dependent on the institution for benefits (Barton, 1975).

The *enduring* aspects of dependency relationships, Barton claimed, create a greater need for consensus on basic values. Another problem with due process expansions, therefore, is that it encourages an adversarial posture and thus heightens conflict. Polarization of interests is particularly detrimental for clients because they are dependent. Formalism, Barton argued, undermines and interferes with these ongoing relationships because it increases the distance between the bureaucracy and the clients it serves. In the case of schools, Goldstein noted that:

Indiscriminate reliance upon the judiciary and the adversary process, as the means of resolving many of the most routine problems arising in the classroom would arrive at a time when divisiveness in schools is already high and school administrators are searching for mechanisms that encourage unity rather than factionalism within the school community (Goldstein, 1976:642).

Threatened by the prospect of replacing bureaucratic norms with judicial standards, some legal reformers went beyond the assertion that formalism is a costly way for clients to redress institutional conflict. They defended bureaucratic norms. The fear was that due process requirements would restrict the exercise of administrative and professional expertise (Wilkinson, 1976). The judgments of "experts" were defended as the appropriate governing decisions over due process standards.

Among those who have been cautious and critical of due process expansions, however, there are mixed views on the extent to which due process standards would impact upon bureaucratic behavior. Not all critics prefer bureaucratic norms, and some are skeptical of whether bureaucracies will comply with judicial standards. Predicting compliance problems with *Goss*, David Kirp observed that "the mismatch between procedural ideals and bureaucratic norms will, in the end, be attributable either to a failure of communication by the Court or to the selective perceptions of school officials" (Kirp, 1976:864).

The differentiation between judicial norms and bureaucratic norms may create relative autonomous authority structures that work against compliance. Marc Galanter has suggested that the mere existence of judicial norms creates a sphere of relative autonomy for bureaucratic norms.

The same differentiation that provides autonomy to elaborate and apply legal doctrine without external dictation works not only on the law, but also on other large institutional complexes as well. The sphere of industrial life, education, science, and so forth, also enjoy some measure of autonomy and thus become relatively impervious to legal controls. In short, the price paid for the differentiation and relative autonomy of the legal order is its loss of leverage on these other institutional spheres sufficient to control behavior there by means of legal doctrine (Galanter, 1979:19).

Clashes between different sets of institutional norms may result in more than noncompliance. Joel Handler's study of welfare bureaucracies (1966) concluded that more stringent due process requirements only result in more informal and less visible forms of institutional regulation. Routinization of due process requirements by institutions serves to mask their discretionary actions. This finding suggests that forcing proceduralism on institutions may in the end advance bureaucratic discretion rather than control it.

Whether bureaucratic norms are threatened or strengthened by encroaching judicial standards continues to be an open question. These critics, nonetheless, shared the view that due process protections achieved little or no substantive gains for the clients. It was suggested that rudimentary due process protections are hollow or at best symbolic rights (Galanter, 1976b). *Goss v. Lopez* was pointed to as an example. Some critics argued that proceduralism is inherently flawed because the scope of procedural protections is limited to factual determinations and does not substantially address the standards that are applied to these determinations. In addition, critics objected to the particularism of adjudicative facts. That is, they argued that such facts only deal with individual circumstances and do not raise questions about substantive policy issues (Wilkinson, 1976; Kirp, 1976). Similar arguments were made about the rudimentary elements of due process protections extended under *Goss*. Critics maintained that these types of protections did not address substantive issues such as the grounds for suspension, and therefore "*Goss* affords the appearance of due process without sufficient substance to guard against the extremes of administrative discretion it was intended to address" (Lufler et al. 1976:15).

In addition to support for institutional alternatives, which came from these diverse perspectives on due process and bureaucratic behavior, the issue of violence within institutions influenced the development of alternative institutional grievance mechanisms. Laura Nader and Linda Singer observed that "the most dramatic example of grievance mechanisms created as a result of violence has occurred in prisons" following the Attica prison riot in 1971 (Nader and Singer, 1976:283). Grievance procedures established in 1972 at the California Youth Authority (a prison for youth offenders) are examples of some of the first attempts to institutionalize informal grievance procedures (Ford Foundation, 1978). The process consisted of three stages. First, inmate grievances were mediated by a committee comprised of elected inmates and prison staff. If an agreement was not worked out through mediation, the dispute was arbitrated by the prison administration. This decision could then be appealed to a tripartite arbitration panel, which "included one person chosen by the grievant, one person chosen by the administration, and a volunteer outside arbitrator" (Nader and Singer, 1976:258; also see Keating, 1975). By 1975 all of the youth prisons in California had adopted this type of grievance procedure (Ford Foundation, 1978).

Perhaps due to the somewhat less violent nature of conflict in schools, administrators in these institutions have been less willing to implement a grievance procedure like the one developed by the California Youth Authority. However, labor-management mediation techniques used in community mediation and institutional grievance procedures elsewhere are presently being taught to students, and there have been experiments with informal dispute processing in schools.[11] The virtues of labor-management mediation, extolled by the advocates of community mediation, were incorporated into the arguments for informal institutional grievance mechanisms. Mediation was praised as both a mechanism for channeling complaints and containing conflict without destroying the fundamental institutional relationship.

From Rights to Relationships: The
Neighborhood Justice Movement

While institutional grievance procedures were developing, the movement to apply labor-management mediation techniques to social conflicts expanded into the area of minor criminal and civil dispute processing. In fact, from the late 1970s to the present most government-funded programs have focused on minor disputes (Ray, 1983). Reformers have linked minor civil and criminal disputes (consumer, family, and neighborhood) by again emphasizing ongoing relationships rather than civil or criminal rights. The relationship between seller and consumer is obviously different from the more intimate ongoing relationship in domestic cases, neighborhood disputes, or disputes between friends. Nonetheless, informal dispute-processing reformers emphasize that the continued contact (past, present, and future) between disputants is a reason for introducing mediation (see Chapter 1).

This shift toward preserving the ongoing relationships of consumers and families is a response to rights movements. The consumer rights movement, for example, fought to prohibit business from using Small Claims Courts, and to provide consumers with legal assistance to advise them of their rights (see Moss-Magnuson Warranty Act 1975). Numerous studies have found that Small Claims Courts function as collection agencies and that nonjudicial complaint-handling systems are ineffective (see Yngvesson and Hennessey, 1975; Best and Andreasen, 1977; Ruhnka and Weller, 1978; Nader, 1979; and Silbey, 1984). The power imbalance between individuals and small businesses or corporations is a fundamental barrier to equal justice in minor civil disputes. Consumer rights advocates, such as those who participated in the debates over the Dispute Resolution Act, argued that in order to increase *access* to equal justice consumers need better protections and better complaint-handling systems.[12]

In the area of family law, efforts to establish legal protections for battered women and greater equity in divorce and child support agreements are some of the major achievements of the women's rights movement. Research findings indicate that most instances of domestic violence are not reported, and that women need additional protections at all levels of the dispute process. In terms of voicing the problem, Raymond Parnas found that "even to a greater extent than police response to intra-family violence, the court response depends largely on the expressed or apparent desires of the victims" (Parnas, 1970:594). However, both police and court intervention into intra-family conflicts fail to provide adequate protection (Meyer and Lorimor, 1977) or enforce the legal rights of women (Connick, Chytilo, and Person, 1980). Shelters for battered women and victim compensation programs developed to address the problems women face when seeking outside help and expressing their claims (see Martin, 1976). Women's rights activists have challenged the role of law enforcement officials and sought better legal protection and assistance for battered women (see Connick, Chytilo and Person, 1980 discussion of class action suits against police departments and Family Courts).

The use of labor-mediation techniques in related party disputes have been criticized on grounds similar to those raised by civil rights activists in the community relations area. First, William Felstiner and Lynne Williams (1979) argue that labor disputes are substantially different from personal disputes. Unlike personal disputes labor disputes arise periodically according to contract negotiations. Personal disputes cannot be contained until the next "contract renewal." Secondly, labor mediation is an impersonal process. Conflict is expressed indirectly through representatives, and the personal feelings between labor and management are not as crucial in contract negotiations as they are in personal disputes where the parties represent themselves (Ibid.:240–241). On the basis of these two differences between labor and personal disputes, critics suggest that labor management techniques are not able to draw out the underlying issues in interpersonal disputes. If this is so, then the claim that mediation is a preventative measure because it addresses underlying issues may not be valid.[13] Neither of these criticisms, however, suggests that social relations should be transformed. The objections to the labor model focus narrowly on technique, leaving unquestioned its purpose—to preserve relationships.

Cost-saving justifications for minor dispute mediation are broader than traditional measurements of institutional efficiency, because they include a calculation of the social costs of *conflict prevention*. It has been claimed that diversion programs, in general, would reduce court case loads and expedite case processing, thus reducing court costs and costs to the parties (Johnson et al., 1977). More specifically, LEAA claimed that mediation services would help lower criminal court case loads, backlogs, and the costs of appealing a case or those resulting from delay (LEAA, 1979). LEAA's cost-saving argument, however, was not simply a monetary one. It claimed that mediation, as a preventative measure, would reduce the social costs of conflict. Domestic violence, simple assaults, unarmed battery, or minor vandalism and neighborhood harassment were defined by LEAA as essentially social problems that could not be resolved effectively by requiring the parties to define their interests in terms of legal rights. Reformers have maintained that diversion of such cases to mediation would permit a focus on underlying issues (Aaronson et al., 1977). Because the emphasis in mediation is not on factual determination of guilt or innocence, justice in this context means agreements tailored to individual circumstances and the needs of the parties' relationship.

CONCLUSION

It is important to clarify that although the informal dispute resolution movement is a reaction to rights movements, some law reformers have cautiously participated in the alternatives movement because they too are somewhat convinced by the argument that informal negotiation may avoid the problems of using the legal system where an ongoing relationship exists. In spite of efforts to secure greater legal resources for consumers and victims of domestic conflict, law reformers remain frustrated with the legal process. The time, money, and psychological costs for claimants who use the legal system still present problems for achieving access to courts. One might argue that in fact because these barriers remain, even those who have pursued a rights-orientated strategy for minor disputes have become partially sympathetic to the central thesis of the alternatives movement: conflict in continuing relationships is best dealt with in an informal setting.[14]

The politics of legal resources in this period are complex. The unusual coalition that banded together in Congress to establish a national policy on dispute resolution was a mixture of conservative legal elites and reluctant but persistent grass roots community organizers. Those who have joined the alternatives movement from the law reform group did not appear to have abandoned their fight for access to courts. In a period of conservative reform, however, the reluctant liberals in this coalition went ahead and joined conservatives, while still maintaining that access to courts might contribute to reducing the imbalance between parties in a negotiation outside the courts. That is, the position that the force of law may simply be necessary to achieve satisfactory nonjudicial settlements (see Mnookin and Kornhauser, 1979) allowed liberals to support alternative dispute resolution without fully abandoning rights movements. The politics of this coalition are rooted in a struggle that takes two views of the politics of rights (Scheingold, 1974). One is against expanding rights and the other is against relying on rights alone. Both views were present throughout the 1960s and early 1970s. By the mid-1970s, however, the former gained the upper hand. The national policy on dispute resolution is, therefore, the combined efforts of conservative and liberal forces to retreat from the politics of rights with the establishment of institutions to preserve ongoing relationships.

NOTES

1. One of the first informal minor dispute programs was established by the American Arbitration Association in Philadelphia in 1968. The program used labor management mediation techniques in the area of community conflict (Stulberg, 1975).

2. For a detailed description of these programs see McGillis and Mullen, 1977. Also for a description of the Columbus program see LEAA, 1974; Boston program see Snyder, 1978 and Felstiner and Williams, 1979 and 1980; Miami program see Dellapa, 1977. LEAA also funded several other programs between 1971–1972.

3. AFSC published a newsletter, similar to the ABA Special Committee on Resolution of Minor Disputes, to serve as a directory of minor dispute programs, to provide information on research in the field, and, unlike the ABA newsletter, to serve as a forum for criticizing the court-based approach to alternatives (*The Mooter*, 1977–1980).

4. A number of national organizations concerned with alternative dispute resolution formed around this time. Largely because of funding problems many of these organizations were short lived. The AFSC, for example, folded due to the lack of funding. The National Institution for Dispute Resolution (NIDR), established in 1983 with its major funding from the Ford Foundation and the Hewlett Foundation, serves as one national networking organization for the field. See National Institution for Dispute Resolution (1984) for information on organizations in the field.

5. Congress did not appropriate funds for the Dispute Resolution Act, nor has the Reagan Justice Department moved to do so. The Act expires in 1985, but the ideology of informalism lives on and is embraced by the Reagan Administration.

6. For example, they supported proposals to make the programs bilingual, "encourage weekend use, discourage overuse by lawyers" (Green, 1978:78).

7. The field of alternative dispute resolution is characterized by a high degree of specialization. Programs have become specialized either according to the particular disputes that they are designed to handle, such as family, neighborhood, prison, or hospital, or according to different dispute-processing techniques, such as negotiation, conciliation, mediation, or arbitration. The field is very fragmented because it has grown out of rather than developed into a tendency toward specialization. Figure 1 does not identify all permutations of alternative dispute resolution, it only presents the broad range of program focus.

8. IMCR does recognize that some community conflicts are inappropriate for mediation (see Nicolau and Cormick, 1972:100–101).

9. Community mediation services developed in the late 1960s still exist today (Stulberg, 1975). They are involved primarily in hearing challenges to government-contracting procedures and settling housing authority disputes. For example, following the Martin Luther King riots in Kansas City, Missouri, the city established the Department of Human Relations with aid from the federal government. This department provided mediation services for racial disputes. By the late 1970s, the department was mainly engaged in reviewing city con-

tracts for affirmative action purposes. Those who continue to support community mediation maintain that it has been successful in facilitating agreements and preventing some social conflicts, such as racial disputes, from reemerging (Ford Foundation, 1978; Nicolau and Cormick, 1972; Singer, 1979).

10. See *In re Gault*, 387 U.S. 1 (1967); *Goldberg v. Kelly*, 397 U.S. 254 (1970); *Morrissey v. Brewer*, 408 U.S. 471 (1971); *Goss v. Lopez*, 419 U.S. 566 (1975).

11. Public schools have also experimented with ombudsman programs, originally developed in this country for government agencies.

12. Stewart Macaulay observed some time ago (1963) that strengthening rights in court might influence out-of-court settlements. Laura Nader also concludes access to "court for parties of unequal power could itself shape opportunities for satisfactory settlement without the exercise of legal authority. . . . Expanding judicial relief for minor claims leads to better nonjudicial solutions" (Nader, 1979:284).

13. IMCR maintains that mediation can draw underlying issues out and although mediation is not equivalent to a counseling session, they believe mediators who they train are given sufficient materials on counseling techniques to be used particularly during caucus sessions with the individuals.

14. Some feminist organizations have recently taken exception to this view (see National Center on Women and Family Law, 1984).

Part III

THE NEIGHBORHOOD JUSTICE CENTER

CHAPTER FOUR

Institutionalizing Voluntarism

The political factions in the alternatives movement are united by a shared approach to judicial reform that has been correctly identified as a shift in policymaking "away from a reliance on penalties and toward greater use of incentives in the implementation of public policy" (Brigham and Brown, 1980:7). Participation and enforcement in most mediation programs is called "voluntary." The policy of informalism relies on the incentive structure of ongoing relationships. Although this incentive structure is seen by reformers as the primary force for resolving related party disputes, reformers are interested in firming up incentives.[1] For example, the Ad Hoc Panel on Dispute Resolution, cosponsored by the Department of Justice and the National Institute for Dispute Resolution, suggests that:

If alternative methods of dispute resolution are to gain widespread acceptance, incentives will have to be found both to establish appropriate programs and to use them. Theoretically, the best incentive would, of course, be that the mechanism dispenses better justice. . . . Nonetheless, it is likely that there will be resistance to these new vehicles. Incentives will have to be developed for lawyers and clients alike to ensure the acceptance and use of alternatives to litigation (Ad Hoc Panel on Dispute Resolution, 1984:19–20).

In this chapter I argue that the degree of institutional coercion over the parties and the level of institutional dependency on the judiciary play a larger role in structuring the relative autonomy of individuals or communities in the implementation of this reform than is recognized by the incentives approach. That is, institutional coercion and dependency affect the role of the community and the courts in *defining* what conflicts are appropriate for mediation and in *controlling* the dispute process. The degree of institutional coercion or the level of dependency are not merely quantitative measures. Qualitative differences in the social and political power of mediation institutions and their clients, and qualitative power differences between neighborhood justice centers and courts must also be taken into account.[2]

In 1977, LEAA commissioned a study on neighborhood justice center models that focused on the issue of coercion, but largely failed to examine the *relationship* between the power of the process (institutional capacity) and the power of the parties over the process (disputants' capacity). Instead, three models were presented on a continuum of noncoercive to coercive dispute processes (McGillis and Mullen, 1977).

One model, Richard Danzig's "community moot," stresses that "the community itself can potentially bring pressure to bear upon disputants for maintaining agreements" (McGillis and Mullen, 1977:26). This is the model "grass roots" advocates support. Supporters of the "community moot" argue that citizen dispute resolution programs must "return ownership of disputes to the people through an informal process" (*The Mooter*, 1977:3). The parties are brought together before "a third party *who has no authority to impose any state sanctions whatsoever*" (Wahrhaftig, 1977:13).[3]

In contrast to the "community moot," Eric Fisher's (1975) "community court" model recommends that these tribunals "be provided by the legislature with exclusive jurisdiction over certain minor disputes and have the authority to impose sanction when necessary" (McGillis and Mullen, 1977:29). This is a coercive and highly institutionalized model for informal dispute processing.[4] The third model, Frank Sander's "dispute resolution center," is considered an "intermediate option." The

Sander model "would not transfer coercive sanctioning authority from the formal system to the tribunal, as in Fisher's model, but would offer binding arbitration services as a means of enforcing decisions and would therefore be more authoritative than Danzig's "community moot" (McGillis and Mullen, 1977:28). These dispute resolution centers would be operated by the government (Sander, 1976, 1977).[5] Chief Justice Warren Burger, former Attorney General Griffin Bell, the American Bar Association, the American Arbitration Association, the Institute for Mediation and Conflict Resolution, and LEAA all supported this model (McGillis and Mullen, 1977:28, 31). The Sander model was very influential in shaping the Dispute Resolution Act, and it continues to be the dominant program model (see Ray, 1983).

Following the 1976 National Conference on the Causes of Popular Dissatisfaction with the Administration of Justice, the federal government took a leadership role in promoting alternatives and adopted the Sander model. Of the three Justice Department initiated experiments in neighborhood justice, the Kansas City program most closely conformed to the Sander model.[6] It was a government-sponsored program.[7] It did not have the sanctioning authority to impose fines or imprisonment. Both parties were required to "voluntarily" sign a prior consent form agreeing to have their case heard by a lay citizen trained in mediation. Awards for personal damages, injuries, or property loss could be made through binding arbitration if the parties were unable to reach an agreement in mediation.

Although it is now undisputed that the majority of mediation programs are court based rather than community based (see Ray, 1983), there has been little attention to the policy implications of court-based "alternatives" beyond the early debates between grass roots advocates and those supporting court-based programs (see Chapter 3). By examining dimensions of coercion and non-coercion some of the policy implications of this reform movement become apparent.[8] What does implementing public policy through incentives mean? How independent (or dependent) are neighborhood justice centers from the courts? Is the public policy shift to incentives and voluntarism merely a symbolic reform that extends the state's role in minor dispute processing? In addressing these questions, the policy implications of establishing informal adjudication of minor disputes receive critical attention.[9]

The answers to these questions might come after examining a case study based on the Kansas City Neighborhood Justice Center. This program not only is an example of the implementation of national policy guidelines on dispute resolution, but it is also characteristic of the majority of mediation centers that have been established. In adopting an "intermediate" model, the staff of the Kansas City Neighborhood Justice Center (herein referred to as the Neighborhood Justice Center) "concur[red] that coercion does exist, not only in these cases [referrals from the police, judges, and prosecuting attorneys] but in other referrals as well" (Arps et al., 1978:172). "Our postulation," they said, "relies upon the thought that community referrals, walk-ins, and peer referrals depend upon a power context which is somewhat more subtle—some party wishes to end the conflict and through some sort of persuasion, the disputants decide to participate. Consequently our staff believes that the difference is one of degree, and we believe that distinguishing between coercion of these types is difficult at best" (Ibid.). I argue that this "sort of persuasion" produces a policy that in turn institutionalizes voluntarism.

RESEARCH METHODS AND DATA COLLECTION

The research for this study is based on a combination of case analysis (mediation and court cases), interviews, and participant observation. The case analysis includes data on all cases referred to the Neighborhood Justice Center from March 1978 through January 1979. In this ten month period 591 cases were referred to the Neighborhood Justice Center.[10] Data were also collected on a control group of 545 related party cases filed in the prosecutor's office of the Kansas City Municipal Court.[11] These cases represent the universe of minor related party cases[12] filed in the prosecutor's office during a ten month period.[13] The complaint forms from the prosecutor's office contain the complainant's description of the dispute and the arrest charge. These forms were also used to determine whether a prior relationship existed between the disputants. Additional information on arrest and disposition of the court control cases was obtained from Municipal Court records and police records.

The Neighborhood Justice Center staff and referral sources were also interviewed (police, judges and prosecutors from the municipal court, court administrator, defense counsel, legal aid attorneys, and pre-trial diversion personnel).[14] These interviews focused on the history of informal dispute process experiments in Kansas City,[15] program implementation, and evaluations of the Neighborhood Justice Center as an alternative to other dispute processes in the community. In addition, the interviews with police, prosecutors, defense counsel, and judges addressed issues dealing with minor related party disputes: how much time is spent on these cases; how frequently do they come in contact with these disputes; what type of case dispositions result from their dealings with these disputes; and how are these cases treated in the judicial system as compared to diversion programs[16] and the Neighborhood Justice Center.

This is not an ethnography of minor dispute processing or a study of mediation strategies.[17] I did observe a number of mediation hearings and talked with mediators about the hearing process to get some sense of the dynamics of mediation. I also observed the screening and referral processes in the prosecutor's office. This included observation of the prosecutor's role and the role of the Neighborhood Justice Center staff in the referral process. In this same period I observed proceedings in all of the seven courtrooms in the municipal court. Finally, I rode along with police officers to see how they responded to disturbance calls and made referrals to the Neighborhood Justice Center.

THE SETTING

During the initial planning stages of the Neighborhood Justice Center, a "target population" was identified. The area selected was essentially the jurisdiction of a police patrol division. The approximately 53,000 people who live in this area, live in what is considered high-density housing, with less compact sections. The area patrolled by this police division is racially mixed, but it has one of the highest percentages of black residents in the city. The median family income is described as moderate to low, with the highest percentage of people living below the poverty line in this part of the city. These socioeconomic characteristics practically describe what was widely referred to as an area hit hard by urban riots in the 1960s, and later became the location of urban renewal housing projects. It is a highly transient population and as a result there is a sense of fragmentation rather than community.

Defining "community" in terms of the jurisdiction of a police division is only the beginning of the story about how neighborhood justice is structured. Other than serving as a symbol for LEAA's approach to planning "community justice," this definition does not describe the actual jurisdiction of the neighborhood justice program. Instead, the scope of the *referral network* is a more precise definition of "community." It extends beyond local community groups and citizens in the area. In fact, most of the cases referred to the Neighborhood Justice Center were from outside the target area (see Sheppard et al., 1978).

Home for the Neighborhood Justice Center was a third floor office in a modern bank building located on a main boulevard in the target area. Its five full-time staff members were city employees. As a city program, staff believed that the Neighborhood Justice Center had credibility when dealing with judges and prosecutors and even to some extent with the police. The Kansas City Police Department is not governed by the city, but as a result of earlier Progressive municipal reforms, it is governed by a state board. The affiliation with city government contributed to the Neighborhood Justice Center's own institutionalization. Most of the staff members had previous work experience in social service areas such as juvenile pre-trial diversion programs or in the social work field. None of the staff members was a lawyer.

The staff and a small advisory board[18] were responsible for recruiting people from the community to be trained as mediators. Most of the fifty mediators who were recruited also had work experience in the social service areas (social work, primary and secondary education, and social service positions in city government). Only a few of the mediators were lawyers. The racial composition of the mediators is similar to that of the clientele, mixed between blacks and whites with a smaller percentage of hispanics.

Half of the mediators received forty hours of training from the American Arbitration Association and the Institute for Mediation and Conflict Resolution; the other half participated in a training program run by the staff. Mediators were not full-time employees. They were notified of a hearing and if they participated they were compensated on a flat-rate basis, fifteen dollars per hearing. Hearings lasted anywhere from one hour to four hours depending on the number of witnesses and parties, and the nature of disputed issues.

The majority of people referred to the Neighborhood Justice Center, both complainants and respondents, were between the ages of nineteen and thirty-nine. Of the complainants, 68 percent are female, 32 percent are male; 40 percent of the respondents are female, 60 percent are male. In the two largest categories of disputes, harassment and assault (46% of the cases), women are complainants against men; this accounts for the higher percentage of female complainants.[19] The racial composition of disputants is mixed between blacks (49%) and whites (46%), with a smaller percentage of hispanics (5%). Only 12 percent of the cases referred to the Neighborhood Justice Center involved interracial disputants.[20]

A large majority of clients have an annual income below $6,000. Many of these individuals are unemployed.[21] Occupation data are difficult to analyze because of the way it is recorded, and educational information on clients was not ascertained. However, since most of the disputes are between parties in ongoing relationships (78% of the cases are domestic, friends, and neighbors),[22] it appears that disputants are usually from the same social class.

GETTING CASES: THE REFERRAL AND
INTAKE PROCESS

There are three general eligibility criteria for referring cases to mediation: (1) the disputants should have an ongoing relationship; (2) disputes should be of a minor civil or criminal nature; and (3) cases should show a potential for successful mediation. Referral agents, rather than general guidelines, however, determine what is sent to mediation. The Neighborhood Justice Center depends first upon the willingness of court and police personnel to make referrals and secondly they rely upon the legitimacy and power of these actors to channel clients to the Neighborhood Justice Center; encouragement to participate in what is formally called a voluntary program.

The referral network heavily depends on the criminal justice system to identify and channel complaints. Table 1 shows the source of case referrals. The criminal justice system (police, prosecutor's office, and municipal court judges) provides the largest percentage of referrals, with 67 percent of the Neighborhood Justice Center's cases coming from them alone. Referrals made by non-criminal justice sources made up the remaining 33 percent of the program's caseload. Non-criminal justice referral sources included: private attorneys, Legal Aid, city agencies, private agencies, and the largest percentage of them are self-referrals (see Table 1).

The largest single source of referrals is the prosecutor's office. These referrals are the result of a clerk's hearing in which the complainant tells her dispute to a prosecutor at the warrant desk. Whether he issues an arrest warrant for the accused or not, the prosecutor may make a referral to mediation; this means that both arrest and non-arrest cases are referred from the prosecutor's office (see discussion below). A staff member from the Neighborhood Justice Center sat in the prosecutor's office and listened to the complaints also. He usually did not get involved in the decision to issue an arrest warrant unless the prosecutor asked for his advice. Only after the prosecutor had decided to divert the case to mediation did the neighborhood justice staff person give the complainant information about mediation and the Neighborhood Justice Cen-

Table 1
The Neighborhood Justice Center Referral Nework*

	Judge[a]	Police	Prosecutor[b]	SCC[c]	Attorney[d]	City Agency[e]	Private Agency[f]	Walk-ins	Other	Total
Percentage of total	15%	20%	32%	.5%	5.5%	9%	4%	12%	2%	100%
Number of cases	88	117	187	3	32	50	24	70	9	580

*All cases referred to the Neighborhood Justice Center from March 1978 to February 1979; data missing for 11 cases.

[a] Municipal judges referred 80 cases, and 8 cases were referred from juvenile court.

[b] City prosecutors referred 185 cases, and 2 cases were referred by the county prosecutor.

[c] Small Claims Court.

[d] Private attorneys made 15 referrals, and 17 cases were referred by legal aid attorneys.

[e] The referrals include disputes from the Housing Authority, welfare and social services, Action Center, and Animal Control.

[f] The Landlord Association referred 20 cases, and 4 cases were referred by the Better Business Fureau.

ter. Once the complainant agreed to take her dispute to mediation, the Neighborhood Justice Center would attempt to
locate the respondent and get him to make the same agreement to participate in a mediation hearing.

The police were the second largest referral source. In most
cases, these referrals were made as a result of a domestic or
neighborhood disturbance call to the police department. The
police gave the disputants information about the Neighborhood Justice Center and advised them to go to mediation and
work out their problems. A neighborhood justice staff person
held meetings with police officers to educate them about the
uses of mediation and on occasion a staff member would ride
along with the police to serve as an on-the-spot screener for
neighborhood justice referrals. Many of the police referrals were
arranged by the staff person who went on patrol with the police.

Municipal court judges made 15 percent of the referrals to
the Neighborhood Justice Center. Most of these referrals were
made on the recommendation of the prosecutor, yet some were
based on the judge's decision that mediation was a more appropriate forum for handling the problem. In either case, these
referrals were made on a pre-conviction basis. If the parties
agreed to go to the Neighborhood Justice Center and reached
an agreement in mediation, the prosecutor would recommend
to the judge that the charges against the defendant be dropped.

The Neighborhood Justice Center held several public events,
such as open houses, and developed media campaigns adver-
tising their services to the legal organizations, community
groups, and citizens. Literature mailings went to private organizations, such as landlord associations, the local Chamber
of Commerce, and the Bar Association. Newspaper coverage of
the opening, attended by former Attorney General Griffin Bell,
gave the Neighborhood Justice Center public exposure, which
played a role in developing referral sources outside the criminal justice system. However, as Table 1 indicates, the number of referrals for any one of these sources was rather small.

What Disputes Are Referred to Mediation?

The *types of minor related party disputes* referred to the Neighborhood Justice Center are shown in Table 2, along with the referral source. Harassments and assaults were the disputes most frequently referred to the Neighborhood Justice Center (63%). Most of these cases (88%) were referred by actors in the criminal justice system (prosecutor, police, and judge). Other referrals from the criminal justice system included disputes involving disorderly behavior by neighborhood children, complaints about dogs, complaints about the upkeep of a neighbor's property, and disputes over small debts. Fewer harassment and assault cases were referred by non-criminal justice sources (see Table 2). Landlord/tenant (25%) and consumer disputes (17%) constituted the largest number of cases referred from these agencies.

Tables 3 and 4 provide information on the *kinds of relationships* between disputants in these related party cases. Table 3 shows the type of relationship between parties in complaints referred from the criminal justice system. And Table 4 shows the types of relationships between parties in complaints referred by non-criminal justice sources. Disputes involving people in domestic and neighborhood relationships constituted the largest category of criminal justice referrals to the Neighborhood Justice Center (81%) (see Table 3). The largest percentage of complaints referred by non-criminal justice agencies were between neighbors (29%), with landlord/tenant disputes as the second largest group (24%) (see Table 4).

Disputes with *arrest charges pending* constituted only 21 percent (124 cases) of the cases referred to the Neighborhood Justice Center. Nine of these cases were referred by a non-criminal justice agent, the remaining were diverted by the criminal justice system. The cases with arrest charges pending came mainly from referrals by a judge (65%). Table 5 shows the numbers of criminal justice referrals that refused to participate in a mediation hearing, those that went to a mediation hearing, and cases that were conciliated, distinguishing

Table 2
Disputes Referred to the Neighborhood Justice Center

	Judge	Police	Prosecutor	SCC	Attorney	City Agency	Private Agency	Walk-ins	Other	Total
Harassment	22	24	53	–	6	10	–	4	1	120 (21%)
Assault	47	39	43	–	4	2	–	4	1	140 (42%)
Destruction of Property	3	6	15	1	1	4	1	–	–	31 (5%)
Children[a]	7	15	14	1	2	7	–	6	–	52 (9%)
Custody/ Visitation	–	4	7	–	–	2	–	–	–	13 (2%)
Dog/ Property[b]	5	13	14	1	3	9	–	11	2	58 (10%)
Debts[c]	1	6	24	–	4	6	–	8	2	51 (9%)
Consumer	–	1	3	–	7	6	–	17	–	34 (6%)
Landlord/ Tenant[d]	2	6	9	–	4	3	23	13	1	61 (11%)

Employer/ Worker	1	–	4	–	–	–	–	5	–	10 (2%)
Other	–	2	–	–	1	1	–	–	–	4 (1%)
Total	88	116[f]	188[g]	3	32	50	24	68[h]	7[i]	574 (100%)

[a] Disputes between adults over the behavior of neighbors' or friends' children.

[b] Complaints about dogs, upkeep of property, and noise.

[c] Disputes involving withholding of property, debts, or bad checks.

[d] In 12 cases the landlord filed a complaint against a tenant and in 48 cases the tenant filed a complaint against the landlord.

[e] In all 10 cases workers filed the complaint against their employer.

[f] Data missing for 1 case.

[g] Data missing for 1 case.

[h] Data missing for 2 cases.

[i] Data missing for 2 cases.

[j] 11 observations missing with 6 cases missing data as indicated above.

117

Table 3
Type of Relationship between Disputants in Cases Referred[a] from the Criminal Justice System

	Domestic	Friends	Neighbors	Consumer	Landlord/ Tenant	Employer/ Worker	Other	Total
Harassment	42	11	40	2	2	–	2	99 (26%)
Assault	77	7	36	1	1	1	2	125 (33%)
Destruction of Property	9	3	11	–	1	–	–	24 (6%)
Disputes involving Children and Custody/Visitation	14	–	31	–	–	–	–	45 (12%)
Dog/Property	–	–	31	–	–	–	1	32 (8%)
Debts	18	9	2	1	–	–	1	31 (8%)
Consumer	–	–	–	4	–	–	–	4 (1%)
Landlord/Tenant	–	–	–	–	17	–	–	17 (4%)
Employer/Worker	1	–	–	–	–	4	–	5 (1%)
Other	2	–	1	–	–	–	–	3 (1%)
Total	163 (42%)	30 (8%)	152 (39%)	8 (2%)	21 (6%)	5 (1%)	6 (2%)	385

[a]Total of 392 criminal justice referrals (judge, police, prosecutor), 7 cases missing.

Table 4

Type of Relationship between Disputants in Cases Referred[a] by Non-Criminal Justice Agents

	Domestic	Friends	Neighbors	Consumer	Landlord/ Tenant	Employer/ Worker	Other	Total
Harassment	5	6	9	-	-	-	-	20 (11%)
Assault	8	1	2	-	-	-	-	11 (6%)
Destruction of Property	3	1	2	-	-	-	-	6 (3%)
Disputes involving Children and Custody/Visitation	2	2	13	-	-	-	1	18 (10%)
Dog/Property	-	-	25	-	-	-	-	25 (14%)
Debts	8	5	-	3	1	-	1	18 (10%)
Consumer	2	-	-	28	-	-	-	30 (17%)
Landlord/Tenant	-	-	-	1	43	-	-	44 (25%)
Employer/Worker	-	-	-	-	-	5	-	5 (3%)
Other	-	-	1	-	-	-	1	2 (1%)
Total	28 (16%)	15 (8%)	52 (29%)	32 (18%)	44 (24%)	5 (3%)	3 (2%)	179 (100%)

[a]Complete Data missing for nine cases.

Table 5
Participation* in NJC for Arrest and Non-Arrest Cases Referred from the Criminal Justice System

	Arrest				Non-Arrest			
	Judge	Police	Prosecutor	Total	Judge	Police	Prosecutor	Total
Refusal[a]	7 (9.5%)	4 (15%)	5 (38%)	16 (14%)	4 (13%)	47 (56%)	66 (40%)	117 (45%)
Conciliation[b]	-	-	-	-	4 (13%)	7 (8%)	33 (20%)	44 (17%)
Hearing[c]	67 (90.5%)	23 (85%)	8 (62%)	98 (86%)	5 (38%)	30 (36%)	66 (40%)	101 (38%)
Total	74 (100%)	27 (100%)	13 (100%)	114 (100%)	13[e] (100%)	84[f] (100%)	165[g] (100%)	262 (100%)

*Aside from the 3 categories of participation shown here, it should be noted that in 3 cases, all from the prosecutor's office, NJC made referrals to another agency and in 11 cases NJC was unable to contact the respondent.

[a]Refusal means one or both parties failed to participate, in nearly all cases the respondent refused to participate

[b]Conciliation means either that the complaining party withdrew the complaint or a reconciliation was reached between the parties. The NJC played a primary role in conciliating 10 cases; the remainder were conciliations between the parties apart from direct NJC "intervention."

[c]Hearing means that the parties participated in an NJC hearing.

[d]One judge referral is missing.

[e]Of the 13 judge referrals categorized non-arrest, 8 came from juvenile court and it was not apparent in the NJC case file whether there had been an actual arrest; this was also the case in the 5 remaining cases.

[f]There were a total of 89 police referrals without arrest, in 5 cases the NJC was unable to contact the respondents.

[g]There were a total of 174 prosecutor referrals without arrest, in 6 cases the NJC was unable to contact the respondents and 3 referrals were made by the NJC prior to a hearing.

the cases that had arrest charges pending from those that did not involve an arrest charge. A large number of the prosecutor referrals are cases not involving an arrest charge. This is also the case with police referrals. Only 7 percent (13 out of a total of 187 cases) of the prosecutor referrals were cases involving an arrest charge. Police referrals that involved an arrest charge represented 23 percent (27 out of 116 cases) of police referrals. In both settings, the prosecutor or police officer issued an arrest warrant, but recommended that the parties take their problem to the neighborhood justice program first.

VOLUNTARINESS, CONSENT, AND COERCION IN REFERRALS

Selling the concept of mediation to *both* parties, particularly the respondent, is the key to getting disputants to participate in the neighborhood justice mediation process. If we examine the *impact of different referral sources* (criminal justice system and non-criminal justice) on the selling process we find that *incentives and sanctions to participate in mediation are not solely within the disputants' relationship, but in fact they are also structured by the referral source*. In addition, the presence of state sanctions, such as an arrest charge, function as an "incentive" to participate in a mediation hearing.

Table 5 shows that a mediation hearing was held in 86 percent (98 cases) of the cases referred by the criminal justice system where an arrest charge was involved. In those cases referred by criminal justice agents *without charges* pending, the Neighborhood Justice Center was far less successful at getting the parties to participate in a hearing. In these cases, without an arrest charge pending, only 38 percent (101 cases) participated in a hearing, 17 percent (44 cases) were conciliated prior to a hearing, and 45 percent (117 cases) refused to participate.

Participation increases when there is greater contact between the disputants and criminal justice officials and the Neighborhood Justice Center staff screener. For example, police referrals most often involve contact with both parties, but the staff screener does not have the advantages of direct contact with the disputants. Prosecutor referrals, the largest percentage of all referrals, originate with one party going to the warrant desk in the city prosecutor's office. In 93 percent (165 cases) of prosecutor referrals, no arrest had been made and no charges filed. Of these cases 40 percent reached a Neighborhood Justice Center hearing, 20 percent were conciliated prior to it, and in 40 percent one party refused to participate (see Table 5).

A slightly higher percentage of prosecutor referrals *without* charges have a mediation hearing than similar cases referred by the police. The staff screener in the prosecutor's office is able to intercept one party and use persuasion tactics such as the suggestion that mediation offers a type of counseling that may help the parties resolve their problems. This type of intervention encourages the complainant to pursue the mediation program instead of "lumping it" (Galanter, 1974). In addition, the prosecutor's office sent letters to the respondent in about half of the cases they referred. These letters stated that if the respondent participated in the mediation program "the City Prosecutor will waive prosecution on this charge." If in ten days the respondent does not contact the Neighborhood Justice Center to schedule a hearing date, the letter said that "the case will be considered for full prosecution." In cases where the respondent refused to participate, the Neighborhood Justice Center did *not* notify the prosecutor, and the city prosecutor did not reconsider the case for prosecution. One might argue that because there was no actual force behind the implied sanction stated in the letter, the letter was not a coercive mechanism to induce participation. Yet, when we look at all non-arrest cases referred by the prosecutor's office and the police, we find that those who received the letter appeared more willing to conciliate an agreement, if not participate in a hearing, than those who did not receive the letter.

In commenting on the issue of coercion at the referral stage, one analyst of a similar community mediation program observed that: "where a judge, a prosecutor, or a court clerk firmly believe in the propriety of a referral of the case to an informal process like community mediation it is *inevitable* that subtle coercive pressure will be brought to bear against the individuals to accept the alternative" (Snyder, 1978:782; emphasis added). The "inevitability" of subtle coercive pressure to participate in these programs deserves more serious consideration than simply noting that it is part of the process of public informal adjudication, particularly when the type of cases being referred to mediation would probably not have received quasi-judicial scrutiny. The consequence is an informal dispute-processing policy for order maintenance problems. Disputes not warranting prosecution are channeled by police and prosecutors to an informal public tribunal. Persuasion and subtle pressures to participate in these quasi-judicial settings are part of the policy and process of "alternatives."

Indeed, where persuasion by staff screeners and the subtle coercion of criminal justice officials does not exist, compliance with a referral to mediation is lower. Table 6 shows what happened to cases referred by non-criminal justice sources without arrest charges. Only nine cases with arrest charges pending were referred by a non-criminal justice source. Six of the nine cases with charges pending went to a mediation hearing. In three cases the respondent refused to participate. Of the remaining cases without charges, in 17 percent (28 cases) mediation hearings were held, 33 percent (55 cases) were conciliated prior to a mediation hearing, and 50 percent (83 cases) refused to participate. Fewer non-criminal justice referrals participated in a mediation hearing than criminal justice re-

Table 6
Participation in NJC for Cases Referred from Non-Criminal Justice Agents[a]

	SCC	Attorney	City Agencies	Private Agencies	Walk-ins	Other	Total
Refusal	2	17	23	9	29	3	83 (50%)
Conciliation	–	5	12	12	25	1	55 (33%)
hearing	1	5	9	2	9	2	28 (17%)
Total	3	27	44	23	63	6	166 (100%)

[a]This table only includes cases where there was no arrest.

ferrals when an arrest was not involved (17% compared with 38%).

However, a larger percentage of conciliations were made in non-criminal justice cases (33%) than in criminal justice referrals (17%). The type of disputes referred by non-criminal justice agents (landlord/tenant, neighbors complaining about dogs running loose or the upkeep of a neighbor's property, and certain consumer cases) appear to reach some type of resolution prior to a mediation hearing. Half of these conciliations were made with the assistance of neighborhood justice staff; the remaining conciliations were reached by the parties without direct staff intervention. It is difficult to determine the effect that the relationship between the parties has on the tendency to conciliate because in these cases the type of dispute is itself associated with the type of relationship. Although a larger percentage of non-criminal justice referrals were conciliated with substantially fewer hearings, in 50 percent of the cases, one party refused to participate, as compared with criminal justice referrals without charges pending where 45 percent refused to participate.

When we look at the effect of disputants' relationships on participation we find that about the same percentage of neighbors (in cases without charges referred either by the criminal justice system or by other agents) refuse to participate as those who actually do participate in hearings. In cases where a closer relationship between the parties existed, a larger percentage of criminal justice referrals participated in hearings than in cases referred by non-criminal justice agents. Although the relationship between referral source and participation when controlling for domestic disputes and disputes between friends is not statistically significant, more criminal justice referrals of this type participated in hearings. In cases where the relationship between disputants is that of consumer/seller, landlord/tenant, or employer/worker, more non-criminal justice referrals were conciliated and more cases reached a hearing. However, more disputes of this type were referred by non-criminal justice agents than from the criminal justice system. These findings suggest that the type of relationship between parties in cases without charges pending is

Table 7

Participation in NJC for Cases Where the Complainant is an Individual and the Respondent is an Organization

	Debts	Consumer	Landlord/ Tenant	Employer/ Worker	Total
Refusal	–	11	15	1	27 (50%)
Conciliation	1	12	9	2	24 (44%)
Hearing	1	1	1	–	3 (6%)
Total	2	24	25	3	54 (100%)

not the sole determinant of participation in mediation. Disputants who were friends or in domestic relationships are more likely to go to mediation if they have been referred by either the police or prosecutor.

In cases where the complainant is an individual and the respondent is an organization, 6 percent participated in a hearing, 44 percent were conciliated, and in 50 percent of the cases the organization refused to participate (see Table 7). The disputes were mainly consumer complaints against a seller or tenant disputes with an apartment-management organization. Conciliation in landlord/tenant cases was most often a property settlement between the parties, worked out by the Neighborhood Justice Center, and an agreement that the tenant would move out. Few cases of an individual complaining against an organization were mediated because the organizations usually insisted on using their grievance procedure and following their policies for handling complaints, both of which business maintained were not subject to mediation. Perhaps the most voluntary acts of refusal occur in these instances. The inequality in bargaining power between an individual and an organization is great (Galanter, 1974). In these cases, when the influence of the mediation program on efforts to conciliate are unsuccessful, the complaint is usually referred to Small Claims Court (see Best and Andreasen, 1977:702; Nader, 1979).

The lack of statutory jurisdiction over specific types of disputes and the lack of authority to require mediation makes alternatives, like the Neighborhood Justice Center, almost entirely dependent upon how court officials and the police exercise their discretion over minor disputes. Compliance with a referral to the Neighborhood Justice Center is influenced by the way subtle coercive sanctions of the "official remedy system" serve to modify the "voluntariness" of participation. To dismiss the significance of institutional sanctions and incentives on decisions to participate in mediation by labeling them as "inevitable," deflects from an analysis of the role of the state in informal dispute-processing policy. Indeed, subtle forms of managing official discretion and processing conflict are essential to the existence of informal public tribunals such as the Neighborhood Justice Center.

THE MEDIATION PROCESS

Mediation at the Neighborhood Justice Center is a blend of two distinct dispute processes: mediation and arbitration. Parties submitting to mediation must sign a "voluntary submission form" consenting to have their dispute heard by a third party mediator *and* agree to participate in arbitration if an agreement is not reached in mediation. The mediators will arbitrate a dispute if they feel the disputants are unable to develop a consensual agreement through mediation.[23]

The so-called hybrid of mediation/arbitration has been characterized as a technique that fuses the "consensuality" of mediation with the "finality" of arbitration (Stulberg, 1975). The combination of mediation and arbitration into one dispute process may create a conflictual role for the third party intervenor, as Sander notes:

Effective mediation may require gaining confidential information from the parties which they may be reluctant to give if they know that it may be used against them in the adjudicatory phase. And even if they do give it, it may then jeopardize the arbitrator's sense of objectivity. In addition it will be difficult for him to take a disinterested view of the case—and even more so to *appear* to do so—after he has once expressed his views concerning a reasonable settlement (Sander, 1976:122).

It may be true that an arbitrator's impartiality is impaired if she participates in confidential caucuses with the disputants under the auspices of a mediator. Instead of retaining the formal distinction between mediation and arbitration, which emphasizes differences between the authority of an arbitrator to make a binding decision and the tools of persuasion available to the mediator who merely recommends a solution, together they function to transform the mediation process into a more proactive type of intervention than pure mediation implies.

The result of blending mediation and arbitration is that at the Neighborhood Justice Center few cases are actually arbitrated. Out of the 235 first mediation hearings held 93 percent (218 cases) resulted in consent agreements, 5 percent (12 cases) were arbitrated awards, 1 percent (2 cases) involved both a consent agreement and an award, and in 1 percent (3 cases) the parties walked out of the hearing before an agreement could be reached.[24] The mediators observed that in most cases the knowledge that a third party would decide the disputed issues if the parties were unable to come to an agreement served as an incentive for the parties to reach an agreement "on their own."

Other incentives to reach an agreement through mediation are built into the process itself, such as references throughout the hearing to the state arbitration law for enforcing agreements. Rituals, such as requiring disputants to sign a weapons affidavit, administering an oath of neutrality to the mediators, and notarizing agreements, gave disputants the impression that "the state was at arm's length." These symbols of authority are external to whatever sanctions exist within the disputants' relationship (e.g., desire to maintain future relationship with one another) prior to a hearing, and as such, they serve to structure the process in which consensual agreements are made.

The principal therapeutic technique underlying neighborhood justice mediation is similar to behavioral contracting,[25] a method for structuring a bargaining process between disputants that focuses on developing a contractual agreement regarding future behavior toward one another. As a form of therapy, behavioral contracting attempts to "structure reciprocal exchanges by specifying who is to do what for whom, under what circumstances. [It] therefore make[s] explicit the expectation of every party to an interaction and permit[s] each to determine the relative benefits and costs to him of remaining within the relationship" (Stuart et al., 1976:230).

Implicit in the theory of behavioral contracting is the assumption that the parties are equally situated in their ability and position to bargain over future behavior. Contracts negotiated in the counseling sessions usually specify contingencies for nonperformance of the contract and include positive incentives or motivations for compliance with the agreement. The disputants are guided toward clarifying their expectations of each other and then negotiating a plan for future interactions. The four conditions most often included in Neighborhood Justice Center agreements were: (1) regulations for future situations of disagreement, (2) promises to refrain from using abusive language and actions, (3) promises to drop charges if they are involved, and (4) promises to avoid actions to one another in the future. Less than a fourth of the agreements contained property damages or debts settlements.

The Neighborhood Justice Center agreements differ in some respects for behavioral contract models in that mediation is at best a limited type of counseling. The neighborhood justice mediation sessions were most often one shot attempts to reorient the disputants' relationship. Few contracts contain contingencies for nonperformance or explicit incentives to reward compliance, although they often provide for some type of monitoring by the staff, such as the handling of financial or property transactions or calling the program office at a specified time to notify them of how the agreement is holding up.[26] These provisions are limited monitoring efforts and their enforcement is also limited. In cases where an agreement to pay damages is not fulfilled, the party may seek enforcement of the agreement in civil court. This situation occurred only once and the agreement was upheld. But the enforcement of behavioral provisions, such as an agreement not to assault or harass the other party or spend more time at home, is reliant on policing by the parties.

The process of "self-policing" (American Arbitration Association, 1978:46) is in part tied to the effectiveness of therapeutic intervention by the third party. When behavioral contracting was first tested in juvenile/family counseling, researchers felt that more detailed contracts would be more effective in structuring compliance. However, recent behavioral contracting studies with juvenile/family members conclude that the specificity of the contract is not the primary factor in ensuring fulfillment of the contract. Instead, researchers have found that "the outcome of negotiation often depends upon a mediator's skill in assuming responsibility for shifts in positions of the bargainers" (Stuart and Lott, 1972:169).

The Neighborhood Justice Center mediation hearings perform this type of proactive function by offering disputants a rationale for reaching a consensus without losing face or assuming guilt. The technique is used to structure the negotiation process and reduce adversarial feelings so that the agreement can be integrated into the natural environment of the parties' relationship.[27] Individuals, assisted by mediators, seek to reach an agreement on how to restructure their future behavior to avoid or prevent conflict. Disputes such as violence against women, neighborhood quarrels, and landlord-tenant problems are reduced to individual problems. The social and economic factors in these disputes are depoliticized or ignored. The process of conflict resolution is internalized by this form of participation.

The intermediate approach to coercion in community mediation models characterizes binding arbitration as the coercive element. Assurance in informal dispute processing that the agreement is binding, however, is a symbolic reference to legal authority. The coercive aspects of incentives and rewards are apparent in the referral process and the process of negotiating an agreement. The enforcement of behavioral agreements is part of the process of making contracts and is dependent on sanctions the parties can use in their relationship. Legal recourse is formally available to ensure compliance. In cases where property is not the disputed issue and the party violating the agreement has not committed an unlawful act, such recourse is a symbolic form of authority that serves to internalize order through the process of participation and self-policing.

CONCLUSION

The ideology of delegalization is an attempt to reconstruct a socio-legal rationale for adjudicating minor disputes. An examination of official sanctions and incentives to participate in mediation suggests that disputants are more likely to participate in mediation when there are strong ties with the official remedy system. Official exercise of discretion has a major role in the operation of the referral network and in the activation of the hearing process.

The expansion of informal adjudication and the construction of a rationale to legitimize minor dispute processing are results of the reform policy advocating "delegalization." The form of this expansion must be understood in terms other than the mere volume of disputes diverted to neighborhood justice programs. Admittedly, few cases are diverted, particularly those with arrests, yet the purpose of this case study is not to determine how *effective* neighborhood justice programs are at drawing cases out of court or absorbing disputes from the community. Instead, we have analyzed the degree of coercion and institutional dependency of the Neighborhood Justice Center.

The type of disputes that are referred to the Neighborhood Justice Center are order maintenance problems that the criminal justice system deals with routinely. Within the decentralized management model, minor disputes are channeled into appended tribunals that emphasize therapeutic intervention by trained lay citizens. Conflict in this setting is absorbed into a rehabilitative model of minor dispute resolution. The creation of a tribunal to mediate these disputes in an individualized therapeutic style signifies a transformation in order maintenance policy that extends the scope of judicial authority. It expands the state's role in identifying and channeling order maintenance problems.

NOTES

1. Institutionalization of alternatives is foremost on the agendum of the Ad Hoc Panel on Dispute Resolution. Although the Panel's report endorses the incentives approach, the report also notes that: "Some suggest that judges need increased statutory authority to invoke this broader use of alternatives. Certainly, these examples add more weight to the suggestion that society pay for options to the court just as it pays for the courts" (Ad Hoc Panel on Dispute Resolution, 1984:23). According to this perspective, the "cost" of alternatives would be absorbed by the state instead of by those disputants who choose to use alternatives.

2. Maureen Cain and Kalman Kulcsar make a similar point in their analysis of dispute theory. They argue that one assumption of dispute theory is that "participants may differ in power or in strategic skill," but qualitatively the participants are identical. And these "differences in power [according to dispute theory] are capable of being equalized: more money, more knowledge, more organization, even more experience, may be given to the weaker party, and then the difference would disappear" (Cain and Kulcsar, 1982:406).

3. Mediation is viewed by the grass roots citizen dispute resolution reformers as a forum of organizing and empowering communities. See Christie, 1977; Shonholtz, 1977; and Wahrhaftig, 1978. For a contrasting view of mediation and community see Johnson, 1978.

4. Although this model was not adopted in the alternative dispute resolution program of the 1970s, aspects of its statutory and institutionalized features are now given more serious attention by reformers.

5. The essential characteristics of the Sander model were present in the early informal dispute resolution programs funded in part by LEAA such as: the Columbus Night Prosecutor Program (LEAA, 1974), the Rochester American Association Community Dispute Services Project in 1972 (Stulberg, 1975), the Miami Citizen Dispute Settlement Project in 1974 (Conner and Surette, 1977), and the New York Institute for Mediation and Conflict Resolution Dispute Center (established in 1970 by a grant from the Ford Foundation and later funded by LEAA in 1975). See McGillis and Mullen (1977). The Boston Urban Court Program (1975) is another example of the application of the Sander model that was supported by a private nonprofit foundation, modeled after the Vera Institute of Justice, called the Justice Resource Institute (Snyder, 1978; McGillis and Mullen, 1977).

6. Initially the two other neighborhood justice centers were variations of the Sander model, but differed somewhat once they were established. For example, the Los Angeles program, sponsored by the Los Angeles Bar Association, was not well integrated into the court system and relied on media advertisement and community groups for drawing cases to the Center. This program had the fewest number of cases as a result. It has been described as similar to the Danzig community moot in terms of the level of coercion employed to get cases (Sheppard et al., 1978). The Atlanta program, on the other hand, was very well integrated with the court system, but unlike the Kansas City Neighborhood Justice Center, it mainly operated out of civil court. The Kansas City program was the only pilot neighborhood justice center that used arbitration as well as mediation.

7. The Kansas City Neighborhood Justice Center was administered by the Community Service Department, a department in the city manager's office.

8. The terms "coercion" and "non-coercion" are not used to imply a dichotomy between the existence or absence of force. Rather, the analysis offered considers penalties and incentives as a dynamic in the style of adjudication and third-party intervention in dispute processing.

9. Research efforts in this area have involved building models for alternative dispute processing rather than examining the policy implications of such reforms. As a result, the relationship between recent reforms in minor criminal and civil adjudication and the type of legal policy such reforms promote has received little critical attention by social scientists. Exceptions to this are Abel (1979, and 1981), and Hofrichter (1982).

10. I selected the Kansas City Neighborhood Justice Center for a case study of informal dispute processing, because it best represents the national policy on alternatives and the majority of informal dispute programs that have been established replicate the main characteristics of this neighborhood justice center. This of course is not to suggest that the findings from this study are applicable to all neighborhood justice centers. The Kansas City Neighborhood Justice Center closed in September of 1980 due to a city policy not to re-fund LEAA programs once federal money ran out. According to the Director of the Community Services Department, the KCNJC was not closed because of its relatively low case load, rather it closed along with two other LEAA funded programs. The city manager's office said that the concept of community mediation will be retained and mediation services will be available in the Human Relations Department.

11. My initial plans to conduct a random assignment study were abandoned because the Neighborhood Justice Center did not want to lose potential cases by diverting them through a court-tracking study. The court control group is a matched sample of related party cases filed in the prosecutor's office. Approximately 10 percent of all the municipal court non-traffic cases came from the prosecutor's office, the remaining general ordinance summons are police arrests.

12. Related party cases were identified by using complainant files in the prosecutor's office. The court and police records do not indicate the name, address, or any other information about the person who brought the complaint. Therefore, the total number of related party cases in the court is not available. Only those complaints filed in the prosecutor's office can be identified as related party cases. The following categories were used to construct an initial sample of related party case control group: the parties had the same last name but lived at different addresses; same last name and lived at same address; same address but not the same last name; and they were neighbors. The Neighborhood Justice Center screener in the prosecutor's office was very familiar with Kansas City, and he constructed the "neighbors" category. I found no significant differences in the types of disputes or case dispositions among these four categories. Therefore, in this study they are treated as one group of minor related party cases.

13. I drew a sample of prosecutor complaints filed one year prior to the creation of the Neighborhood Justice Center to see if there was any significant impact on the number and type of cases the prosecutor took to court once the Neighborhood Justice Center opened in March 1978. Finding no differences, cases referred in 1977 and 1978 during March, June, August, September, and December are compared with Neighborhood Justice Center cases from March 1978 through January 1979.

14. Interviews were conducted with the Director of the Community Services Department (the department of city government that sponsored the Neighborhood Justice Center), the Director and Assistant Director of the Neighborhood Justice Center, all mediation staff liaisons (police department, prosecutor's office, and Small Claims Court), and several mediators. In the municipal court, interviews were conducted with the City Prosecutor, fourteen of the twenty assistant prosecutors, the Court Administrator, and six of the seven municipal court judges. Also interviewed were the Director of the Municipal Court Division of Legal Aid, one legal aid attorney and two private defense attorneys who regularly practice in municipal court, and the directors of two court diversion programs.

15. The Kansas City Neighborhood Justice Center was identified as one of the most successful in developing a police referral system. A mediation experiment in the police department had been set up by the Police Foundation before the Neighborhood Justice Center was established. That program was short-lived (1974–1975), but it did provide police with some exposure to mediation approaches in conflict resolution. Interviews were thus conducted with former and present Police Foundation staff members who worked on the Interactive Patrol Experiment and who were involved with the Kansas City Dispute Resolution Program. For a discussion of problems with institutionalizing referral mechanisms for informal adjudication programs in the Boston police department, see Snyder (1978). The major impediment to developing a referral relationship with the police, according to Snyder, is the police union. Part of the Neighborhood Justice Center's success in developing a police referral may have been the lack of a police union.

16. Kansas City had two other court diversion programs. One was for youth offenders only, and the other was a first offender program, which required that the offender pay $50.00 for counseling and referral services.

17. See Merry and Silbey (forthcoming) for a discussion of mediation styles and strategies.

18. The original grant from LEAA establishing the Kansas City Neighborhood Justice Center required that an advisory board be created for policymaking purposes. Twenty-three people were appointed to the advisory board by the Mayor, most of whom were representatives of the municipal court judges, legal aids, juvenile court, community relation services, the police department, councilmen, and state representatives. The mediation staff described the advisory board as a body of individuals who were brought together to build support for the Neighborhood Justice Center in the areas that the advisory board members were associated with.

19. Background data is missing for many respondents in cases where the Neighborhood Justice Center was unable to contact the respondent or when respondents refused to participate. Data on the sex of the complainant is missing in 21 cases and in 68 cases for respondents; 19 percent of the disputes are between males, 13 percent male complainants and female respondents, 27 percent between females, and 41 percent female complainants and male respondents.

20. Data on complainant's race are missing in 95 out of 591 cases, and for respondents in 169 cases out of 591 cases (54 of which are

organizations). The breakdown for race of complainant is: 226 whites, 243 blacks, 21 hispanic, 1 Asian, and 3 other; race of respondents is: 169 whites, 175 blacks, 20 hispanic, and 1 other. Computation of party's race for disputes is based on 359 cases: 142 both parties were white; 158 both parties were black; 13 both parties were hispanic; 14 white complainants, black respondents; 19 black complainants, white respondents; 6 white-hispanic; 1 black-hispanic; 3 hispanic-white; the remaining 3 were 1 Asian-other and 2 other-white. See Merry (1979) for discussion of minor dispute resolution among ethnic groups.

21. Income data is self-reported, and in many cases missing, again particularly for respondents who did not complete an intake screening form. For complainants, 308 out of 591 cases are missing income data. In 410 cases where there is complete income data for complaints, 228 (56%) reported 0–$6,000; 117 (28%)—6,000–12,000; 43 (10%)—12,000–18,000; 17 (4%)—18,000–24,000; 5 (1%)—24,000–30,000, and 1 organization. In cases where there is near complete data for respondents, 308 out of 591 cases are missing income data. In 183 (of which 54 are organizations, which do not report income) cases where there is complete income data for respondents, 120 (52%) reported 0–6,000; 65 (28%)—6,000–12,000; 29 (12.6%)—12,000–18,000; 14 (6%)—18,000–24,000, and 1 (4%)—24,000–30,000. These income categories were taken from the intake screening form. According to staff members, these figures tend to underrepresent the number of unemployed and low-income people who are referred to the Neighborhood Justice Center.

22. The relationship between disputants was determined according to how the complainant described the disputant's relationship in the voluntary submission form and the type of relationship recorded by the staff screener on the intake screening form. Of a total of 575 cases: 194 (34%) domestic; 206 (36%) neighbors; 47 (8%) friends; 42 (7%) consumer/seller; 66 (11%) landlord/tenant; 11 (2%) employer/worker, and 9 (2%) other. There were missing data in 16 out of 591 cases.

23. Usually two mediators participate at each hearing, an experienced and an inexperienced mediator. The Neighborhood Justice Center schedules certain mediators to specific kinds of hearing cases, for example juveniles, and attempts to arrange a med/arb combination sharing similar sex and race characteristics with disputants.

24. For the 17 cases that had a second hearing, 12 consent agreements were signed, 2 awards, 1 consent agreement and award, and in 2 cases the parties walked out.

25. See Felstiner and William's (1979) criticisms of applying the labor model of mediation of interpersonal disputes.

26. In only 19 consent agreements one or both parties agreed to seek professional counseling for drinking or marriage problems.

27. For a discussion of the self-policing theories applied to early diversion, see Vorenberg and Vorenberg (1973).

CHAPTER FIVE

Access, Participation, and Order Maintenance

Expanding legal participation is one way the state seeks to mediate social relations in a liberal democracy. The judiciary plays an important role in structuring dispute processes to absorb demands for social justice on the one hand, and to maintain social order and stability on the other hand. The *form* of legal participation is, therefore, an important issue in judicial reform. At least since the organized use of litigation as a form of political participation in the Civil Rights period there has been a significant increase in the amount and scope of legal participation, which judicial reformers see as challenging both the institutional and political limits of adjudication. The way in which the state mediates social relations affects the internal organization of the judicial system and alters the form of legal participation (see Chapter 2).[1] In the area of criminal justice, for example, Maurice Rosenberg observes that: "If we fail to set up new extra-judicial mechanisms, we may be inviting problems of two kinds: a continued influx into the courts of an unmanageably large case load and a continuing inability on the part of citizens to voice legal grievances effectively and inexpensively" (Rosenberg, 1981:479–80). These two pressures have in fact influenced the development of alternative forms of participation in dispute processing.

The dominant approach to reforming legal participation focuses on the structure of individual choices and incentives rather than the social organization of dispute-processing institutions (see Chapter 4). This is also the dominant approach in dispute-processing research. It suggests that disputing and patterns of participation in dispute processes are best understood from the disputant's perspective. Individuals' *perceptions* and *motives* are the central determinants of dispute behavior. Dispute behavior becomes a series of strategic decisions about whether to avoid or redress grievances in different settings.

Specifically, two types of research have adopted this approach. First, there are studies that look at the disputants' psychological motives and goals (Vidmar, 1980; Coates and Penrod, 1981). Dan Coates and Stephen Penrod suggest that there are at least three types of motives that are related to the emergence of disputes: (1) relative deprivation, (2) equity, and (3) perceived control over the situation. Neil Vidmar claims that knowledge of motives enhances our ability to predict what dispute process disputants will choose to participate in and their level of satisfaction with the process and outcome. He further identifies four "choice points": (1) perceiving grounds for a complaint, (2) a decision to express the grievance, (3) a decision to involve a third party in the grievance, and (4) options available to the parties if the third party resolution is not reached, that is, withdraw, ease up, resort to illegal means, or seek additional third party involvement (Vidmar, 1980:408–411). Together the examination of individual motives and their effect on choices to avoid or act on grievances may tell us something about the psychological dimension of legal participation.

The second type of research focuses on "choice processes" (Sarat, 1976; Miller and Sarat, 1981). Choice processes essentially are decisions disputants make at various stages in the life of a grievance. Laura Nader and Harry Todd (1978) identified these stages as: grievance, conflict, and dispute (also see Merry, 1979). William Felstiner, Richard Abel, and Austin Sarat (1981) also suggested that there are three stages, which they identify as naming, blaming, and claiming. Richard Miller and

Austin Sarat (1981) call their three stages grievance, claims, and dispute. The process of disputing is described as "the creation and revision of perceptions and attitudes about oneself, one's opponent agents, . . . institutions and personnel" (Felstiner, Abel, and Sarat, 1981:651). Movements from one stage to another are "transformations [that] result from these social psychological processes and are themselves responsible for some of them" (Ibid.).[2] Such studies suggest that *social psychological* processes are key to understanding why individuals, at certain stages in disputing, participate or drop out of the process.

Critics have pointed out that these studies focus too narrowly on individual choices and perceptions to build an adequate sociological theory of dispute processing (Snyder, 1981; Kidder, 1981; Cain and Kulcsar, 1982). In fact, research using this approach has become even more "reductionist" (Kidder, 1981:721) with an increasing emphasis on the genesis of disputes. From this research perspective, the mobilization of law is largely determined by individual choice to initiate a complaint. Courts and extra-judicial dispute processes are depicted as passive institutions, reacting to citizen complainants (see Black, 1973). The treatment of legal participation is limited to the perspective of private citizens using public authority on their own behalf (Zemans, 1983).[3] This approach minimizes the role of the state in organizing dispute forums and the role of the judiciary in structuring forms of legal participation.

Much of the research on alternatives is premised on another dualism, which is equally problematic: informal versus formal (see Chapter 1). To a large extent, the ideology of alternatives ignores the similarities between mediation and adjudication. The concept of alternatives tends to define conflict resolution as the function of mediation, and rule enforcement as the function of adjudication. The structure of sanctions and incentives in the disputants' relationship is defined as the source of authority for mediation, and rules are defined as the source of authority for adjudication. Each form of dispute processing has a distinct rather than a similar source of legitimacy.[4]

The point here is *not* that dispute processes are proactive as opposed to reactive institutions. Nor are alternatives formal as opposed to informal dispute processes. These dichotomous descriptions of legal institutions produce a static image of law and society. Instead of beginning from the premise that dispute processes are reactive rather than proactive or that mediation and adjudication are distinct, in this chapter we examine the relationship between legal participation and legal organization in both settings. More specifically this chapter documents similar patterns of participation and nonparticipation in mediation and prosecution of related party cases. The intent is to understand the continuity among forms of dispute processing by examining the socio-legal organization of dispute processes. The concept of the socio-legal organization of dispute processes focuses on the institutional relationship between dispute processes. We might best think of it as a middle range concept in comparison with more macro theories of litigiousness such as social development theories (see Felstiner, 1974 and 1975; Danzig and Lowy, 1975; Grossman and Sarat, 1975), or the micro level theories of dispute behavior, which concentrate on the choices, motives, or goals of disputants.

THE PROBLEM OF PARTICIPATION

The problem of participation is not as simple as the popular myth suggests: that there is too much litigation. In the alternatives reform movement it involves creating dispute processes that both parties will participate in. Getting disputants to police themselves is central to the order maintenance function of dispute processing. Alternatives have been designed to strengthen this function of the judicial system.

A fundamental claim of the neighborhood justice movement is that parties involved in minor disputes are more willing to take their disputes to informal tribunals than to court (see Chapter 1). The major reason cases are dismissed in lower criminal courts is because the complainant does not show up in court. And the single largest group of cases dismissed involve related party disputes (Vera Institute, 1977). The complainant is often the sole source of evidence for the prosecution of a minor criminal charge. In court, the complainant is the *critical party.*

In mediation, however, it is often the "offender" (respondent) who is reluctant to appear. The offender who appears at mediation might subject himself to charges of wrongdoing, thereby placing himself in a vulnerable position. Although both parties must voluntarily participate in mediation, there are few voluntary incentives for the offender. The offender is the critical party in informal dispute processes. Raymond Shonholtz described this situation in his testimony before Congress on the 1980 Dispute Resolution Act.

> . . . the key problem in the judicial system on the criminal side is the participation of the first party, the victim. The problem characteristically of mediation programs is the second party, the quote unquote offender (Shonholtz, 1978:149).

The challenge to the alternatives reform movement is to create a form of legal participation that attracts the critical party.

Studies comparing mediation and adjudication have concluded that disputants who participate in mediation sessions are more satisfied with the process and outcome than are a similar group who go to court (Cook et al., 1980; Davis et al., 1980). What do these findings tell us about mediation as a form of legal participation? Does mediation strengthen the order maintenance function of dispute processing?

Satisfying Clients and Maintaining Agreements

Client satisfaction and recidivism are the two most common indicators used in comparative evaluation studies.[5] Client satisfaction measures variations in client attitudes. Recidivism, as used in these evaluations, measures the effect of mediation on the client's future behavior toward parties involved in the initial dispute. These two measures are related. Positive attitudes toward the mediation process are supposed to produce long-lasting agreements, and thus reduce recidivism. One should be cautious, however, about how to interpret and weigh client satisfaction responses and recidivism measures when evaluating participation in dispute processes.

First, the respondents in these studies include only the clients who *completed* the mediation process and those who got through the court process (Cook et al., 1980; Davis et al., 1980; Felstiner and Williams, 1980). A large group of people who entered the court process or initially accepted mediation but did not participate in a hearing are not included in client satisfaction studies. For example, in one study, in only 56 percent of the referred cases did both parties actually participate in a mediation hearing (Davis et al., 1980). Those who initially agreed to participate, either by signing a voluntary submission form (mediation) or filing a complainant application with the prosecutor (prosecution), but failed to appear at the hearing stage were not interviewed. Defendants who failed to appear in court were also not interviewed. The study concluded, nonetheless, that "the process of mediation is viewed more positively than the court process, both by the complainants and by defendants" (Ibid.:64). Complainants who went to mediation "felt they had received more attention and had greater opportunity to participate" than complainants who went to court (Ibid.:50). Of the complainants who went to mediation 73 percent said they were satisfied with the outcome of their case, while only 54 percent of the court control groups who were interviewed said that they were satisfied with the outcome (Ibid.:51). The defendants who participated in mediation were also satisfied more often with the outcome of the case than the defendants who went to court with the outcome of the case (compare 77% to 67%) (Ibid.:56). In response to the question of whether complainants felt they had an opportunity to tell their story, 94 percent of those who participated in a mediation session said yes, while only 56 percent who went to a court hearing said yes (Ibid.). In response to this same question, 90 percent of the defendants interviewed who went to a mediation hearing said they did have an opportunity to tell their side of the story, while only 44 percent of the defendants in the court control groups said they had a chance to tell their story (Ibid.:55).

This oversight accounts for the tendency to conclude that mediation programs are successful when only those who choose *to participate* in a mediation session are interviewed. Such research fails to explore the significance of the choice *not to participate* after entering the process. Favorable neighborhood justice center evaluations seem to support one claim made by the alternatives movement: those who participate in mediation favor it because they feel they play a larger role in shaping the process and determining its outcome than do court participants.[6] However, these studies fail to address another claim, one perhaps even more basic to the reform movement, namely that there is a *demand* for mediation services.

Second, random assignment of related party cases into control groups (court cases and mediation cases) creates another problem for client satisfaction studies. In one study, participants in the court control were asked in the beginning whether they would voluntarily agree to participate in mediation or not (Davis et al., 1980). In an effort to create a matched control group (see Zimring, 1974:231), the study may have created certain expectations about each dispute process. The authors themselves note that among "complainants who had not expressed an interest in participating, the difference in satisfaction with the outcome was far less marked; 78 percent were satisfied with the outcome in mediation, versus 65 percent in court. Thus, resolution of their cases, the lack of participation afforded them by the court *process* seems to have adversely affected their satisfaction with the court case *outcomes*" (Davis et al., 1980:53).

The process of "selling" mediation itself may influence client satisfaction. Research on client satisfaction measures suggests that "satisfaction can be viewed as a discrepancy score between what people expect and what they actually get" (Gutek, 1978:51). Those who had a prior interest in mediation but were placed in the court control group were less satisfied with the court process. It is also possible that those who agreed to mediation *and* actually participated in a hearing had a stronger proclivity to favor mediation.

Finally, research on maintaining agreements reached in mediation and upholding adjudicated decisions does not support the claim that a more "participatory" form of dispute processing leads to lower recidivism.[7] Davis et al. concluded that "referral to mediation was no more effective than the prose-cution process in reducing the actual incidence of subsequent hostilities serious enough to provoke calls to the police or new arrests (Davis et al., 1980:73). William Felstiner and Lynne Williams found that in Dorchester the court process may be *more* effective than mediation is in preventing future con-flicts. Their study was based on sixty-nine related party cases that were tracked through the court proceedings and forty-two similar cases that went to mediation. They concluded that "exposure to full court treatment appears to have had a more positive effect than successful mediation for subjects who had committed assaults prior to the 'experimental intervention.' " (Felstiner and Williams, 1980:44).

In sum, the scope of empirical research on alternatives is limited to a survey of those who choose to and actually do par-ticipate in hearings. We know very little about those who be-gin each process but drop out before the hearing stage. The problem of tracking disputants is all the more difficult with those who refuse to participate. Research on dispute transfor-mation may yet offer important insights into decisions not to participate in mediation or prosecution. At this point, how-ever, we only have aggregate data on cases that drop out.

CHANNELING AND ABSORBING CONFLICT IN DIVERSION

Increasing participation in mediation affects decisions to channel and absorb conflicts; it does not merely alter the ex-pectations of those who participate in hearings. The *diversion process* is a critical stage in minor dispute processing. This is so not because it is a careful selection or distribution process, rather like the impact of adjudication decisions on sentencing outcomes (see Feeley, 1979; Myers and Hagan, 1979), the diversion decision determines in part the type of sanctions that will be imposed. In his study of a New Haven lower criminal court Malcolm Feeley concluded that:

There is no clear line which distinguishes sentencing from adjudica-tion. In deciding whether to seek a jail term, ask for a fine, recommend a suspended sentence, press for a plea of guilty, or grant a nolle, the prosecutor goes through essentially the same process. He attempts to establish the "worth" of the case, which in turn dictates how he will treat it. If it is "serious" or "heavy" the arrestee may have to plead guilty and even serve time in jail, but if it is "not worth very much," or if, in more colloquial terms, it is "garbage," "bullshit," or a "meatball," then the defendant may receive a nolle because all agree that it is not even "worth" the time to prosecute (Feeley, 1979:158–9).

Similarly, diversion decisions establish the worth of a case and delineate treatment possibilities. Diversion decisions are a place in the judicial system where conflict is channeled and absorbed.

Establishing the worth of a minor case does not adhere strictly to formal screening criteria. What Feeley tells us about the process of establishing the worth of cases for prosecution accurately describes the process of making diversion decisions: "Although prosecutors and defense attorneys tend to become inarticulate when pressed to specify how they evaluate the 'worth' of a case, they claim to know it intuitively" (Ibid.:159). Similarly, in Kansas City, prosecutors, defense counsel, and judges had a shared understanding about the worth of minor disputes, despite their inability to specify the foundations of this understanding. The city prosecutor was in charge of the largest number of diversion decisions.[8] His role in screening complaints and chaneling them to the court or the Neighborhood Justice Center was seen by all other court personnel as a very unattractive job. Complainants seeking warrants for someone's arrest came to him. Listening to their problems, explaining what goes on in court, and most importantly attempting to settle their disputes, were the routines of the city prosecutor's job.

General guidelines for making diversion decisions were established by the Neighborhood Justice Center: the dispute is between people in an ongoing relationship and it is likely that the problem can be resolved in mediation. When questioned as to what an "ongoing" dispute is, prosecutors and judges first responded with a rather literal definition: a dispute between two or more persons. Although they insisted on retaining the literal definition, further questioning revealed a more specific understanding: domestic disputes, neighborhood problems, and disputes among people who have had some type of prior relationship. An "ongoing relationship" translated into an "interpersonal" relationship.

Most cases that come to the prosecutor's warrant desk involve disputes between people in an interpersonal relationship according to this definition of an ongoing relationship. Prosecutors, defense counsel, and judges estimated that forty to sixty percent of the municipal court cases on the general ordinance docket are interpersonal disputes. This means that of the total cases referred to the municipal court, including cases referred by the police, the single largest type of cases on the nontraffic docket are interpersonal disputes. Only a small number of these cases are diverted to the Neighborhood Justice Center.[9] What factors establish the worth of a minor dispute and determine whether it will be diverted to the neighborhood justice program?

In criminal cases an arrest warrant can be issued if the prosecutor believes probable cause exists that the arrestee committed a crime. One might assume that disputes leading to an arrest are worth more than those that do not result in an arrest because there is a basis for prosecution in the former and not the latter. However, I found that an arrest warrant does not necessarily indicate the value of a minor dispute for two reasons. One is that the prosecutor has no specific criteria for issuing warrants in minor related party disputes. When questioned about the process of justifying a warrant, the prosecutor candidly admitted that in minor disputes of this kind an arrest warrant does not distinguish a case as being worth more than other minor disputes where a warrant is not issued. Cases diverted to the Neighborhood Justice Center with or without arrest charges were probably as worthless as minor cases that went to court. Second, the municipal court judges and prosecutors reported that most related party cases they see in court do not justify a warrant. Minor disputes involving related parties are treated like nuisances, whether there is an arrest charge pending or not. As Feeley observed, "they [lower courts] will not regard as a *crime* that which has typically been treated as a *nuisance*" (Feeley, 1979:8). In the prosecutor's office diversion decisions are not based on whether a warrant is justified, nor in the opinion of the judges and prosecutors in the courtroom is an arrest charge very significant in determining the worth of minor disputes.

The complexity of a dispute does appear to influence the decision to divert disputes to a particular process. For example, prosecutors did not want to get involved with cases with a large number of witnesses, disputes involving long-standing feuds among neighbors or relatives, or some cases where the parties lived together. These cases were seen as prime candidates for neighborhood justice. One prosecutor summed up why prosecutors like the Neighborhood Justice Center for complex related party cases: "Neighborhood justice is really handy because it is like a garbage dump: they will take and deal with cases we simply are not set up to handle. I just like them because they are handy. I wish I could get rid of more garbage that way."

Yet there is a paradox in the "trivialization" of minor disputes (see McBarnet, 1981). Although many prosecutors share the view that complex interpersonal disputes are "garbage" cases, they recognize that most of these cases are not in fact diverted to the Neighborhood Justice Center. Prosecutors and judges find that it is both easier to deal with "garbage" cases than take the time to divert these cases, and "garbage" cases are the work of the lower courts. The established routines for handling minor interpersonal cases remained intact after the establishment of the Neighborhood Justice Center.

Legal Aid attorneys also trivialized related party cases, but continued to handle them instead of diverting them to the Neighborhood Justice Center. As one Legal Aid attorney stated, "Most of them [related party cases] are settled much more quickly and with less hassle by our attorneys. We have been successful at getting complaining witnesses to drop or get defendants to stay away. Most of them would rather get it over quick and forget about it even though it is a conviction; just sign the probation agreement. Whereas neighborhood justice involves a little more time and effort for them. . . . They [the Neighborhood Justice Center] offer an option that is there when we need it; most of the time we don't need it."

Similarly, the judges believed that while the Neighborhood Justice Center could deal with these disputes through extended "conversation" with the parties, so too could the courts. The municipal judges saw their role, in fact, as that of a problem solver rather than a law enforcer. With one exception, the judges all shared a very relaxed and informal style of processing these cases. Remarking on the municipal judges' role as problem solver, one judge said: "In this day and time when people resort to the court to solve all the social ills and problems of their community, many of those ills are hardly significant enough to set in motion a very expensive tax-paid operation called the court system and the so-called criminal justice system but we do serve these problems here everyday."

The exception to this approach is with domestic assault cases. Although many of the prosecutors and, in particular, judges[10] expressed frustration with the adjudication of related party cases, they strongly believed that mediation was not appropriate in most domestic assault cases. This attitude stems from the view that the case itself is serious and the complainant is serious about prosecution. One female prosecutor made this point quite clear in her statement: "I have dealt with too many women in this courtroom who have been in that position [assaulted or harassed] and it is beyond mediation. By the time it gets to the courtroom what they want you to do as the prosecutor and what they want the court to do is keep that son of a bitch away from them. And it is my personal opinion that if you beat up a woman and she wants to press charges she should have the opportunity." Judges said that frequently the relationship between parties in domestic disputes has terminated by the time they reach the court. The women in these cases are seeking legal protection against the men who have assaulted them. Conflict that has escalated to this point is impossible to mediate. Another prosecutor added: "where the blood is hot and the adrenalin is flowing, simple mediation is never going to be considered." Finally, many of the judges did not believe that neighborhood justice program had sufficient resources necessary to properly supervise and counsel domestic disputes. The reluctance of judges and prosecutors to submit battered women cases to mediation removes a substantial number of potential cases from the Neighborhood Justice Center.

Careful decisions as to which minor disputes are appropriate for mediation and which ones should be prosecuted did not result from the creation of the Neighborhood Justice Center. Instead, the traditional routines for handling these cases continue. In cases such as domestic assaults, where the court actors more consciously assess the seriousness of the dispute, this assessment works against a decision to divert the case to the Neighborhood Justice Center.

HEARINGS AND LEGAL PARTICIPATION

Decisions at the hearing stage affect participation also. This stage includes the decision by disputants to participate, and as we discussed in Chapter 4, these decisions are structured by the referral process.

The lower criminal court and the neighborhood justice program share a common class clientele and lower class status. Prosecutors and judges defined a specific community that both the lower court and the neighborhood justice program serve. This community is described by one prosecutor as "agency abusers," comprised largely of unemployed women with children. Another prosecutor's description captures an attitude toward this group that is pervasive among prosecutors and judges in the lower court: "poor white trash; not the black community or the Mexican-American; not even good blue collar." The Neighborhood Justice Center staff describe the people they serve in similar terms and agree that the Neighborhood Justice Center draws on a similar pool of lower class people.[11] Prosecutors, who have private practices in addition to working for the municipal court, said they would never refer their own clients to the Neighborhood Justice Center because of its lower class status.

Table 8 compares the Neighborhood Justice Center docket and the court control group by type of related party disputes.

Table 8
Comparison of NJC and Court Related Party Disputes*

Type of Dispute

	Disorder/ Harass	Assault	Vandalism	Larceny	Trespass	Other[a]	Total
NJC cases	232 (39%)	140 (24%)	32 (5.4%)	56 (9.4%)	1 (.2%)	130 (22%)	591 (100%)
Court cases	75 (14%)	303 (56%)	85 (16%)	13 (2%)	54 (10%)	15 (3%)	545 (100%)

*The description given by the complainant and the arrest charge were used to determine the type of disputes in the related party court control group. The descriptions given by the complainant and the respondent as well as the categories used by the NJC were used to determine the type of dispute for the related party NJC cases.

[a]This appears to be a significantly large percentage of cases referred to the NJC, however, for the purposes of this comparison I collaspsed the civil cases, most of which are non-criminal justice referrals to the NJC, together so that equivalent comparisons can be made with the court control group. The largest percentage of NJC cases in this category are child custody cases

The largest category of Neighborhood Justice Center disputes were disorderly conduct and harassment cases (39%), while the largest category of court disputes were assault cases (56%). Over twice as many assault cases are in the court control group than in the Neighborhood Justice Center comparison (24%). Only 14 percent of the court control cases are disorderly or harassment disputes. Fewer Neighborhood Justice Center cases are disputes involving trespass or vandalism claims. The category of "other" Neighborhood Justice Center cases includes civil disputes between related parties such as consumer/seller, landlord/tenant, employer/employee, barking dog complainants, and custody disputes. These cases were referred by non-criminal justice agents such as city agencies, Small Claims Court, a private attorney, or self-referrals.

The comparison between the Neighborhood Justice Center and court related party disputes changes somewhat if we remove all of the cases referred by non-criminal justice agents and compare only cases *referred by the criminal justice system* (CJS referrals made by police, prosecutors, or judges) to the Neighborhood Justice Center with the lower court cases (see Table 9). Although disorderly and harassment cases still constitute the largest percentage of Neighborhood Justice Center cases (43%), assault disputes are a larger proportion (1/3) of the criminal justice system referrals than they appear to be on Table 8 where assault disputes constitute approximately 1/4 of the entire Neighborhood Justice Center case load. However, even if we only compare criminal justice system referrals to the Neighborhood Justice Center with the court cases, there are more (56%) assault cases in the court group than in the Neighborhood Justice Center comparison (33%).

The Rate of Participation in Hearings

Table 10 compares participation rates in mediation sessions and court hearings. Participation here refers to whether both parties appeared at a hearing. Included in this definition are cases where a second mediation session (17 cases) or a second court hearing (30 cases) was scheduled. Cases that were cat-

Table 9

Comparison of NJC Cases Referred by the Criminal Justice System and Court Cases

Type of Dispute

	Disorder/ Harass	Assault	Vandalism	Larceny	Trespass	Other	Total
NJC cases referred by CJS	168 (43%)	129 (33%)	24 (6%)	33 (8%)	-	38 (10%)	392 (100%)
Court cases	75 (14%)	303 (56%)	85 (16%)	13 (2%)	54 (10%)	15 (3%)	545 (100%)

Table 10

Comparison of Related Party Rates of Participation in the Hearing Process[*]

	CJS Referrals to NJC	Court Cases
Refused to appear[a]	150 (44%)	250 (47%)
Participated in hearing	189 (56%)	287 (53%)
Total	339 (100%)[b]	537 (100%)[c]

[*]This table only compares CJS referrals to NJC with court cases. The rate of participation in an NJC mediation session for all NJC cases is 47% (222 cases), and 53% (254 cases) of all NJC cases did not reach a mediation session.

[a]These are court cases where usually the complainant failed to appear and the case was dismissed for want of prosecution, or a bench warrant or cond forfeiture was issued because the defendant failed to appear. The CJS referrals to the NJC are cases where after a referral one ot both parties signed a voluntary submission form, but one party, usually the respondent, did not show for a hearing.

[b]51 cases are excluded from the total because they were categorized as "conciliations" by the NJC.

[c]8 cases were referred out of court before a hearing took place and therefore were excluded from the total.

egorized as "conciliation" (115 cases) by the Neighborhood
Justice Center are not included in the comparison because there
are no equivalent records for the court comparison. In 53 percent of the court cases a hearing was held with both parties
present, and for the Neighborhood Justice Center cases referred by the criminal justice system a hearing with both parties was held in 56 percent of the cases. These findings suggest that both dispute processes have similar rates of
participation in related party cases.

It might, however, be argued that participation rates alone
are an insufficient basis for comparing the two settings. Those
who claim that mediation allows disputants a greater *role* in
the process and in shaping the outcome argue that mediation
is a more participatory forum than adjudication. This claim is
based on a comparison of the traditional model of adjudication
with an ideal model of mediation (see Fuller, 1971). It has some
empirical support from studies that ask disputants about the
value of participation they assign to each setting. The value
or meaning that disputants attribute to their participation in
either setting is not, however, the issue being addressed here.
Rather here we are interested in whether mediation strengthens the order maintenance function of dispute processing by
attracting both parties. The comparison of participation rates
for each setting in Table 10 suggests that it does not.

In about the same percentage of neighborhood justice related party cases (44%) and court cases (47%) one party refused to participate in a hearing, and therefore the cases were
dismissed.[12] Although in court the complainant is the critical
party whose presence is necessary for state prosecution, in the
Neighborhood Justice Center the respondent is the critical
party. The complainant in most Neighborhood Justice Center
cases (particularly non-arrest cases) first agrees to take her
dispute to the Neighborhood Justice Center. The Neighborhood Justice Center must then search for the respondent and
convince him to participate in a mediation session. Getting *both*
parties in a court hearing or in the mediation session is difficult. Indeed, this issue is a primary concern for mediation
programs around the country. In other community mediation
programs, similar to the Neighborhood Justice Center, one

party (usually the respondent) often refuses to participate in a mediation session. For example, in the Dorchester Urban Court Program, 30 percent refused to appear; the Brooklyn Dispute Resolution Center, 44 percent; the Citizen Dispute Settlement Program in Orlando, Florida, 34 percent; and in the Columbus Night Prosecutor Program, a hearing was not held in 37 percent of the cases, because one party refused to participate (see Ray, 1981). Since these programs are technically voluntary programs, if the respondent refuses to participate in a mediation session the case is closed as far as the mediation program is concerned.

Do participation rates vary for different types of disputes? Table 11 is an analysis of participation rates by type of dispute. For disorderly conduct and harassment cases, there is no difference in participation rates. In 57 percent of these cases referred to the Neighborhood Justice Center by the criminal justice system a hearing was held, and in 56 percent of similar court cases a hearing was held with both parties. The participation rates for vandalism cases are also fairly similar in each dispute-processing setting. Assault cases are the only category in which there is a slightly higher percentage of mediation sessions (64%) than court hearings (51%). However, the effect of an arrest charge on participation rates in the Neighborhood Justice Center may explain this finding. Table 12 compares participation rates for arrest and non-arrest cases referred to the Neighborhood Justice Center by the criminal justice system with the court control group where an arrest charge is present in all cases. The findings show that where arrest charges are pending in a neighborhood justice case there are substantially more hearings (83%) than when no charges are pending (43%). Assault cases constitute the largest percentage of cases referred to the Neighborhood Justice Center with an arrest charge pending (64%, n = 69), with disorderly conduct and harassment cases being the second largest percentage of arrest cases (32%, n = 35). In both types of disputes, if an arrest charge is pending a hearing is held with both parties in 80 percent of the cases.

The rate of participation in mediation sessions is much higher in cases where charges are pending (83%) than the rate of

Table 11

Comparison of Participation Rates in NJC and Court by Type of Dispute*

	Disorder/Harass		Assault		Trespass		Vandalism		Larceny	
	NJC	Court	NJC	Court	NJC	Court	NJC	Court	NJC	Court
Refused to appear	61 (43%)	32 (44%)	41 (36%)	146 (49%)	-	24 (44%)	11 (50%)	38 (46%)	13 (52%)	5
Participated in hearing	81 (57%)	40 (56%)	74 (64%)	155 (51%)	-	30 (56%)	11 (50%)	45 (54%)	12 (48%)	7
Total[a]	142 (100%)	72 (100%)	115 (100%)	301 (100%)	-	54 (100%)	22 (100%)	83 (100%)	25 (100%)	12

*This table only compares CJS referrals to NJC with court cases.

[a]35 NJC cases are excluded because the type of dispute is not one of the 5 main categories of disputes (24 refused to appear, 11 did participate in a mediation session). 15 court cases are excluded for the same reason (5 refused to appear, 10 did participate in a hearing).

Table 12

Comparison of Parti   tion Rates in NJC and Court Controlling
r Arrest Charge

	Arrest Charge		No Arrest
	NJC	Court	NJC
Refused to appear	19 (17%)	250 (47%)	130 (57%)
Participated in hearing	91 (83%)	287 (53%)	98 (43%)
Total	110 (100%)	537 (100%)	228 (100%)

participation in court hearings (53%). A much smaller percentage of disputants in Neighborhood Justice Center arrest cases refuse to participate in a mediation session (17%), compared with the percentage in the court control group where the critical party refuses to participate (47%). This is so because in arrest cases referred to the Neighborhood Justice Center the referral itself is part of a court case disposition. Whether the referral is made by a judge, the police or the prosecutor this seems to be the case (see Chapter 4).

We can also expect a higher percentage of neighborhood justice arrest cases than non-arrest cases to go to a mediation session. Table 12 compares court control cases with non-arrest cases referred to the Neighborhood Justice Center by the criminal justice system. A higher percentage (57%) of neighborhood justice cases without arrest charges pending are dismissed because one party refused to appear for the hearing than in the court group (47%). More court cases (53%) reach a hearing than neighborhood justice non-arrest cases (43%).

This comparison of participation rates suggests that if we look at participation *and* non-participation in dispute processing the critical party is not more willing to participate in a mediation session than is the critical party in conventional adjudication willing to participate in a hearing. A similar percentage of minor related party disputes drop out of the Neighborhood Justice Center and the court hearing process. The alternatives movement may function to widen the dispute-

processing "net" by absorbing more minor conflicts and channeling them to particular forums (see Chapter 4), but the
Neighborhood Justice Center seems to reproduce conventional
patterns of legal participation.

THE SANCTIONS IN THE OUTCOME

In what sense are lower court outcomes different from the
outcomes in mediated cases? Table 13 shows final case dispositions for the court control group. A total of 67 percent were
dismissed either because the complainant failed to appear
(37%), the prosecutor withdrew the state's case (16%), or because the judge dismissed the case (14%). In only 23 percent

Table 13
Court Control Group Case Disposition*

Disposition	Number of Cases
Dismissed	
Complainant failed to appear	197 (37%)
Released by prosecutor	85 (16%)
Dismissed by court	77 (14%)
Bench Warrant[a]	22 (4%)
Bond Forfeiture[b]	31 (6%)
Guilty	125 (23%)
Total[c]	537 (100%)

*These are the final case dispositions. Only 59 cases had more
than one schedualed court appearance.

[a]Bench warrants are issued for cases where the defendant fails
to appear.

[b]Technically a bond forfeiture is not a finding of guilt.

[c]8 cases were referred to other authorities.

of the cases was the defendant found guilty. These dispositions do not vary much according to the type of dispute. In all types of disputes, the largest percentage of cases are dismissed because the complainant failed to appear. The second largest category of dispositions, for all types of disputes, is a guilty finding. There is some variation among types of disputes in this category. For example, the defendant is found guilty in fewer assault cases (20%) than in trespass (34%), disorderly conduct (28%), or vandalism (27%) cases (see Table 14). The two types of disputes most often diverted to mediation (disorderly conduct and assault) constitute the majority of the dismissals in the court control group, while representing a somewhat smaller percentage of guilty dispositions in court.

What type of sanctions are imposed on the defendants in these cases? In the majority of cases (61%), the defendant received an unconditional discharge or a ten day suspended sentence with two months unsupervised probation. Fines are rarely imposed: 16 percent received fines under $50.00 and 5 percent were fined more than $50.00. In 18 percent of the guilty convictions, the judge ordered that the defendant spend some time in jail (see Table 15). Except for those who serve jail time, in this lower court the process of adjudication is the punishment itself in minor criminal cases (Feeley, 1979; and see Ryan, 1981 for a contrasting view).[13]

The Neighborhood Justice Center does not have the authority to impose sentences or fines, but it may award property settlements and money damages. Mediation sessions were held in 235 cases, and 93 percent of these cases concluded with a consent agreement. The terms of the agreement represent the sanctions produced by mediation. The four most frequently imposed sanctions were (1) the promise to refrain from using abusive language and actions, (2) drop pending charges, (3) avoid future contact with one another, and (4) pay property damages or debts. Other than the agreement to drop charges and pay damages, the type of sanctions are mostly behavioral. For example, most consent agreements provide that the parties will never come in contact with each other; if a situation should arise where they do, orderly behavior is required.

Table 14

Court Control Group Case Disposition by Type of Dispute

	Type of Dispute					
	Disorder	Trespass	Vandalism	Larceny	Assault	Total
Dismissed (failed to appear)	25 (35%)	16 (32%)	30 (37%)	2	116 (39%)	189 (37%)
Dismissed (prosecutor released)	8 (11%)	8 (16%)	8 (10%)	3	53 (18%)	80 (16%)
Dismissed (by court)	11 (16%)	4 (8%)	13 (16%)	3	42 (14%)	73 (14%)
Bench Warrant	3 (4%)	2 (4%)	5 (6%)	2	10 (3%)	22 (4%)
Bond Forfeiture	4 (6%)	3 (6%)	3 (4%)	1	19 (6%)	30 (6%)
Guilty	20 (28%)	17 (34%)	22 (27%)	-	59 (20%)	118 (23%)
Total[a]	71 (100%)	50 (100%)	81 (100%)	11	299 (100%)	512 (100%)

[a] 37 cases missing data, and 8 cases were referred to other authorities.

Table 15
Sanctions in Court Cases

Sanctions	Number of Cases
Unconditional discharge, suspended sentence	67 (61%)
Under $50.00 fine	17 (16%)
Greater than $50.00 fine	5 (5%)
Jail sentence (maximum of 6 months)	20 (18%)
Total[a]	109 (100%)

[a]16 cases missing data.

Avoiding future contact is often the primary concern, particularly in assault cases. But a complainant who goes to court often desires some form of protection as well. Typically she wants the judge to issue a peace bond to prevent the defendant from coming near her and her children. The peace bond and the consent agreement requiring disputants to avoid one another are both symbolic forms of protection. Some judges will issue peace bonds on the insistence of the complainant, but warn her that there is no real enforcement mechanism. Only if the defendant is arrested for violating a peace bond will some sanctions be imposed; but the sanction is only the subsequent arrest itself. Little else is likely to happen. Similarly, upholding the consent agreement to avoid one another is not self-enforcing.

In contrast to disputants in lower court, disputants in mediation agreed to the sanctions. Little data exist on how well these agreements hold up compared to adjudicated cases. Recidivism studies are all that is available. Those studies, mentioned earlier, suggest that recidivism is lower for adjudicated cases. However tentative and reliable these findings are, the point is that both approaches to minor disputes rely on the disputants to uphold and enforce outcomes of the dispute process. Satisfactory resolution of these disputes is, of course, less tied to specific remedies (payment of damages) than it is dependent on changes in future behavior.

CONCLUSION

Research on entry into dispute processing must move beyond focusing alone on the concern with access, and begin to identify internal contradiction in the socio-legal organization of dispute processes. Whether in fact participation in dispute processing produces more effective order maintenance, is a question for future research. Clearly there are many intervening variables in the transformation of disputes and the resolution of social conflict that might conceivably have an important impact on order maintenance.[14] Nonetheless, one conclusion of this study is that mediation programs, such as the Neighborhood Justice Center, do not increase critical party participation. Thus even if we assume that there is a correlation between increased participation in dispute processing and more effective order maintenance, the Neighborhood Justice Center does not significantly contribute to enhancing it.

The politics of participation and non-participation can best be understood by examining the ideological and organizational structure of dispute processes. There are internal contradictions in these structures that reveal patterns of participation. A rationalized screening process for minor disputes contradicts the socio-legal organization of the lower courts. The paradox of trivializing related party disputes is that they are not diverted to the neighborhood justice program because they are so "trivial," yet the lower courts handle them because that is what they see as their work. Some cases are nonetheless diverted to the Neighborhood Justice Center. In these cases, participation by both parties is about the same as the rate of participation in lower court related party disputes. The legal organization of alternatives, including the diversion process and the hearing process reproduces the pattern of legal participation in the lower criminal court.

NOTES

1. See Heydebrand and Seron (1981) for a discussion of the rise of administration in the Third Branch and an analysis of administrative reform within the judiciary.

2. The term "transformation" is used in dispute-processing literature in a very general sense to mean change from one *stage* of disputing to another. The conditions under which changes take place are not specified. Thus, the determining factors are unclear (also see Fitzgerald and Dickins, 1981, comments on the use of transformation language). Mather and Yngvesson (1981) include social processes, such as audience participation, in their discussion of dispute transformation (narrowing and expanding), which offers a rich understanding of the context of rephrasing.

3. Literature addressing the issue of mobilization tends to concentrate on the initiatives of citizens (see Zemans, 1983, discussion of the role of citizen-complainants in the legal process), or the abilities of citizens (Galanter, 1974; Grossman and Sarat, 1981:125). Also see Lempert (1976) and Black (1973). This concept of mobilization of the law refers to activities apart from rather than in conjunction with the constraints imposed by legal structures.

4. See Nonet and Selznick (1978) and Fuller (1971) as examples of this perspective. For further discussion of this issue see the literature on legal pluralism (e.g., Galanter, 1979; Engel, 1980) as well as critiques of the concept of legal pluralism (e.g., Santos, 1979; Abel, 1981; Fitzpatrick, 1983).

5. In addition to these measures, the impact of mediation programs on courts has been studied by comparing the costs of mediation with prosecution, and by measuring the impact of mediation programs on court case load and its effect on court services. William Felstiner and Lynne Williams' study of the Dorchester Urban Court program is one of the few reliable cost analyses of mediation and adjudication (1980). They used a court control group of related party court cases similar to those sent to mediation (assault and battery). After constructing court careers for this group, the length of court time was compared with mediation time as were personal costs for both processes. They found that "mediation costs are 2 to 3 times the amount of court costs saved" by diverting a case to mediation (Felstiner and Williams, 1980:42). They concluded that mediation services in Dorchester were most effective in reducing court costs in the area of probational supervision. This finding is supported by the Vera

Institute study of felony diversion in the Brooklyn Dispute Resolution Center (1980). Although the Vera Institute did not do a cost study, they did examine the use of court time and court services. They found that mediation "reduced the system's use of pre-trial detention resources and its use of arresting officers' time for court appearances" (Davis et al., 1980:v). Both studies point out that mediation programs associated with courts may reduce the load on traditional services such as probation and detention, but at the same time mediation creates additional costs such as training new mediators and hiring program staff members.

There is also widespread evidence that mediation programs, particularly those connected to criminal courts, do not reduce court congestion and delay. The small number of cases referred to mediation, though prosecutors and judges are the largest referral source, constitute a fraction of the non-traffic docket in lower criminal courts. The American Bar Association survey of dispute resolution programs found that 51 percent of the existing programs have an annual case load to 500 or less; 35 percent range from 500 to 3,000 cases annually and 14 percent have an annual case load of 3,000 (Ray, 1981). Typically, those programs with the largest case load are affiliated with Small Claims Courts. In Kansas City, I found that municipal court judges, prosecutors, court administrators, and Neighborhood Justice Center staff all agreed that the Neighborhood Justice Center would have no significant impact on the court's general ordinance summons docket (the non-traffic docket). The court administrator, prosecutors, and Neighborhood Justice Center staff said that the annual general ordinance summons case load was approximately 50,000. The computerized court/police records that I analyzed showed that substantially fewer cases are filed annually (28,000 general ordinance summons). Whether we rely on the perceptions of case load or the actual case load count, the Neighborhood Justice Center's annual case load of 841 cases does not significantly impact on court case load.

Court delay in processing interpersonal disputes is yet another basis on which to compare mediation and adjudication. Although in Kansas City the average court *hearing* takes less time (5–15 minutes) compared with mediation (2–6 hours depending upon the number of witnesses), the Neighborhood Justice Center cases are *processed* faster. 62.3 percent (147 cases) of the Neighborhood Justice Center cases are mediated within two weeks of the time they are referred. Only 10.6 percent (57 cases) of the court cases are processed in two weeks or less (see Appendix A). Of course, the total municipal court case load is substantially larger than the Neighborhood Justice Center case load. Only one docket a day (in five courtrooms) is devoted to general ordinance summons. Each docket is one hour and fifteen minutes. The court administrator said that the municipal court did not have a case backlog or any significant delay problems. According to him, general ordinance summons cases are usually processed within six weeks of the arrest time.

6. The Department of Justice evaluation of the three Neighborhood Justice Centers is one such favorable evaluation (Cook *et al.*, 1980). The study provides little documentation or explanation of the selection criteria used to identify court control cases in Atlanta and Kansas City. For example, we do not know whether or not people in the court control groups (Atlanta and Kansas City) were asked if they would voluntarily participate in mediation. Research on how to create matched samples for making comparisons between two programs has suggested that researchers should ask members of the court control group whether they would voluntarily participate in mediation if they were asked to. This type of question is supposed to control for the voluntary requirement of the mediation program, and ensure that those in the mediation group are no more disposed to mediation than those in the court control group (see Zimring, 1974:231). Furthermore, the court control group findings in the Department of Justice study are based on a very small number of follow-up interviews. Of the 107 cases from the Atlanta court and 32 cases from the Kansas City court, follow-up interviews were held with only 42 complainants and 25 complainants respectively. In Atlanta, two-thirds of the complainants interviewed in the follow-up questioning reported that they were "satisfied" with the judge, but only 42 percent felt the handling of their case was "good," while 30 percent said the handling of their case was "poor" (Cook et al., 1980:80). The study did not control for differences in court dispositions (continuances, not guilty or guilty). Of those who participated in a mediation session at the Atlanta Neighborhood Justice Center, 90.6 percent said they were satisfied with the process and 89.4 percent reported being satisfied with the mediator (Ibid.:55). Similar results were reported in Kansas City. In both the court cases and the mediated cases we are given no indication as to what the respondents in the interviews meant by such general evaluations like "satisfied," "good," or "poor." The conclusions of the study in Kansas City were especially vague: "In regard to the manner in which their case was handled in court, the majority of the complainants in Kansas City felt that it was poor, although almost all said it was good or average" (Ibid.:80). Neither study controlled for the influence of court conviction or acquittal on the complainant's evaluation of the court process. It is also unclear how a "majority" of the complainants in the Kansas City control group could evaluate the

court process as "poor" with almost all of the complainants evaluating the court process as good or average. The conclusion that mediation clients were, on the whole, quite "satisfied," is also ambiguous.

7. For a discussion of compliance with mediated versus adjudicated small claims disputes see McEwen and Maiman (1984). This study found that compliance with mediated agreements was significantly higher than compliance with adjudicated agreements.

8. The prosecutors are a very homogeneous group of people. The majority are white males who have been practicing law for five years or less (private general practice mainly, one legal aid attorney, and a few were prosecutors in the juvenile court). All of them work on a part-time contract basis for the prosecutor's office and have a general practice on the side. As a result of changes in office hiring policy and guidelines for reappointment, most of the prosecutors were hired about one year prior to my research. They are all around the same age (30–35) and they often referred to this as an attribute in their working relations (ability to accept criticism, and be flexible in their dealings with defense attorneys and judges they work with).

9. If we look at the number of complaints filed in the prosecutor's office one year before the mediation program was established and compare them with the complaints filed after the Neighborhood Justice Center was created, we find that there is little change in the total number of related party cases that the prosecutor sent to court (see Appendix B). The Neighborhood Justice Center staff claimed that few cases were diverted from the prosecutor's office and from the municipal court because of "turf" battles between the court and the Neighborhood Justice Center. As one staff member said, "the overloaded court system wants to be overloaded—it makes them powerful, gives them control."

10. In contrast to the prosecutors, the judges in the municipal court have served much longer in their positions (9–11 years). Only one judge, previously a magistrate judge, was new to the court. All of the judges are white males, except one black judge, and they are between 50 and 60 years of age. With the exception of one judge, they share a similar style of handling minor disputes. They all describe themselves as problem solvers not adjudicators. The extent of aggravation in assault cases is perhaps the only significance of legal evidence in their opinion. They are extremely frustrated with the diversion treatment programs associated with the court and have little or no confidence that these programs will rehabilitate defendants in assault cases. In speaking with the prosecutors about their attitudes toward their jobs and the people they come in contact with in the municipal court, I found that initially they would describe their work

as a legal job (gathering evidence, presenting it to the court, etc.). However, after a while the prosecutors eventually began describing their jobs as social work jobs having little or nothing to do with legal standards or procedures. The judges, on the other hand, were all very cynical about their jobs, which they described from the beginning as social work not legal work. These differences in perceptions/expectations may be related to socialization.

11. Prosecutors and the judges in Kansas City maintain that a particular community is served by both the Neighborhood Justice Center and the court. A socio-economic description of the Neighborhood Justice Center clients is presented in Chapter 4. Court records, however, do not provide information on the complainant's race, therefore a comparison of court and Neighborhood Justice Center disputants by race is not possible.

Complete information is also not available on the age of the respondents in the Neighborhood Justice Center cases. A comparison of the existing age data with the age of defendants in the court control indicates that the largest percentage of defendants are between 19 and 29 years old. This is similar for the respondents and complainants in the Neighborhood Justice Center (see Chapter 4).

The largest percentage of related party disputes within the Neighborhood Justice Center and court control group are initiated by women against men (see Table A). This is due to the fact that in both the

Table A
Sex of Disputants in NJC and Court Control Cases

	NJC	Court Control
Female v. Male	191 (41.1%)	429 (80.5%)
Female v. Female	125 (26.9%)	16 (3.0%)
Male v. Male	87 (18.7%)	43 (8.1%)
Male v. Female	62 (13.3%)	45 (8.4%)
Total	465 (100%)[a]	533 (100%)[b]

[a]Complete information is missing in 126 cases.

[b]Complete information is missing in 12 cases.

Neighborhood Justice Center and the court control, the largest categories of disputes are assaults and harassments. However, because fewer court control cases are disorderly and harassment cases than are Neighborhood Justice Center cases a larger percentage of the court control cases are female v. male than are Neighborhood Justice Center cases. Also we have more complete information on the sex of court control disputants. This factor may account for the larger number of reported female v. male cases.

12. I was unable to systematically study the reasons why parties referred to mediation did not participate in a hearing after initially agreeing to participate. The Neighborhood Justice Center did not maintain complete files for these cases. However, based on the records that did exist I found that the most common reasons given for not participating in a hearing were: respondent's lawyers advised him to go to court instead; respondent wanted to go to court; respondent did not believe the issue would to to court if he refused to mediate; one or both parties felt mediation was a waste of time; respondent moved; complainant wanted to go to court because she/he believed there was more coercion in the court's decision; and in cases involving department stores or apartments, company representatives refused to participate because they felt the Neighborhood Justice Center lacked legal compulsion, and they wanted the consumer or tenant to use their in-house grievance procedures.

13. The presence of legal counsel has been found to lead to a lesser sentence (Feeley, 1979). According to the judges and prosecutors, defendants and complainants in the Kansas City Municipal Court rarely have a lawyer at the first hearing. In only 59 court cases was there a second hearing, and we have no record on whether defendants or complainants had counsel at either the first or second hearing.

14. Some factors that may affect order maintenance are whether the police were involved, at what stage of the dispute one party called in a third party, did the prosecutor attempt to mediate the case or not, etc. The purpose here is not to determine what factors improve order maintenance, but instead make the point that order maintenance is far more complex than some reform models suggest.

Conclusion

This book is part of a tradition of scholarship on the social phenomenon of dispute processing. It has focused on the movement for alternative dispute resolution, as that movement has been evident in minor criminal and civil related party cases that come to lower courts and neighborhood justice centers. This is one of the manifestations of the movement and a slice of dispute processing that shows alternatives offering a kind of shadow justice. We conclude by calling attention to some of the findings and by pointing out some potential problems confronting this reform movement.

THE FINDINGS

Dispute-processing reforms have played a significant role in the judicial management strategies of the twentieth century. These reforms, often characterized by hostility to the formality of conventional processes, claim to provide informal justice. The principal elements of informal justice link the movement to judicial management strategies. We have seen this in the emphasis on rationalizing dispute processes. As one reformer suggests: "The challenge is to distribute disputes among dispute resolution methods in some rational manner that will contribute to the overall performance of the justice system" (Johnson, 1978:24). This distribution incorporates a new body of disputes often missed by traditional forms of order maintenance and expands the capacity of the state. Thus, the ideology of informalism constitutes an administrative-technocratic rationale for judicial intervention to maintain public order.

Expanding Capacity

Informalism expands the capacity of the justice system to manage minor conflicts and legitimates the extension of state intervention on functionalist grounds. The ideology of informal justice in the neighborhood justice movement is a theory of institutional legitimacy for the order maintenance function of minor dispute processing. The new basis for legitimacy, functionalism, places a special emphasis on the role of participation in conflict management. Participation is viewed as a key to altering behavior, maintaining agreement, reducing alienation and popular dissatisfaction with courts, and increasing the willingness of disputants to use public (informal) dispute processes.

The development of alternatives has maintained a continuity with the conventional practices of minor dispute processing while effecting a change in the scope of judicial capacity. Disputants are more likely to participate in a neighborhood justice mediation hearing when there are strong ties with the official remedy system, such as a referral by a criminal justice agent or when an arrest charge is involved. The coercion and authority of police, prosecutors, and judges are essential elements to the institutional existence of neighborhood justice centers. In so far as those who participate in neighborhood justice mediation hearings are more satisfied with the process and outcomes than those who go to court, alternatives legitimate the processing of minor disputes. Yet, the Neighborhood Justice Center does not seem to increase critical party participation. Minor disputants in related party cases seem no more willing to participate in mediation than in adjudication. These findings suggest that mediation *reproduces* the participation problems reformers sought to resolve with alternatives.

Legitimation

The development of alternatives has also maintained a continuity with traditional legal ideology (formalism) by emphasizing procedural fairness *and* effected a transformation in that legal ideology by establishing a new basis (functionalism) for legitimacy of minor dispute institutions. The nature of the transformation in legal ideology is thus a change *within* the ideology of minor dispute processing and not a complete shift away from legalization as suggested by the term "delegalization."

The alternatives movement has had greater success in legitimating institutions to those who participate in them, than it has in getting minor disputants to voluntarily bring their conflicts to mediation. The nature of the shift from an adversary, formal ideology to informalism should thus be seen as a rationalization of management style rather than a fundamental change in the processing of minor conflicts. The Neighborhood Justice Center is dependent on the exercise of official discretion to divert cases to it and in the activation of the hearing process. Yet enforcing order maintenance relies on the capacity of the disputants' relationship to impose sanctions along with other aspects of the "self-policing" process discussed in Chapter 4. The *form* of state expansion in the concept of alternatives must, therefore, be understood as "state produced non-state power" (Santos, 1980).

The Neighborhood Justice Center is a shadow of conventional adjudication practices. The dependency of these centers on courts for their place and meaning in the legal process and, through the use of official coercion, to provide cases contribute to the proposition that the justice in the neighborhood justice centers is a shadow justice.

SOME OTHER SHADOWS

Alternative dispute resolution, particularly where it is linked to lower courts in the form of neighborhood justice centers, is not only functionally in the shadow of the justice provided by those courts but the future of this movement is also dimmed by a number of developments and considerations. These include the growing professionalization of alternative dispute resolution staff and the consequent abrogation of the informalist/alternative caste, the loss of a social justice component both historically, in the movement itself, and with reference to what is supposed to go on in courts, and the loss of a forum for political action and struggle.

Professionalism

Although empirical studies of civil and criminal adjudication suggest that the threat of "litigiousness" is far less serious than some court reformers have claimed, these findings do not necessarily pre-empt the growth of alternative dispute resolution. The court reformers who fear increasing litigiousness have not gone away, nor has the community self-governance orientation of the movement completely disappeared. Despite the fact that court-based alternatives characterize the dominant orientation of this reform, a struggle *within* the alternative dispute resolution field over resources continues to raise political questions about who shall control dispute processing: professionals, lay-citizens, or disputants.

Initially, the debates between court reformers and grass roots community organizers described the internal politics of this reform (see Chapter 3). Today, however, the main political struggle is taking place within the context of professionalization. Pressure to professionalize alternative dispute resolution is coming from the legal profession as well as mediator organizations, such as the Society of Professionals in Dispute Resolution. Questions of certification and training are now pivotal points in the professionalizing process. Mandatory mediation legislation and the establishment of certification requirements for mediators are two examples of the push to professionalize (see Chapter 2). Both efforts move this reform further toward institutionalizing mediation as another tier in the judicial system.

Rights and Social Justice

The alternative dispute resolution movement is a movement of "anxious professionals and unwilling participants" (Ad

Hoc, 1984:2–3). This is so because substantive demands for social justice have been overshadowed by experimentation with techniques of alternative dispute resolution. This focus on dispute techniques has separated the politics of problem solving from the politics of taking rights seriously. The management style of informal dispute processing in the Neighborhood Justice Center tends to separate rights from their social base in political struggles. Going to court does not always mean arguing about rights in a formal sense. Taking rights seriously can mean taking problem solving seriously. We need to turn our attention to the substantive rights and claims for justice that are expressed in the dispute-processing context. Once we understand that the exercise of rights, making claims of rights, is an expression of social problems (e.g., social and economic inequality), then we can move forward with the view that rights are one context or framework in which social problem solving takes place.

The Arena

The alternatives movement seems to have abandoned an important resource and arena for political struggle—rights and courts. Whether we look to the court-based top down reform exemplified by the Neighborhood Justice Center, or the community-based bottom up reform efforts of the San Francisco Community Board Program, both have adopted strategies that move resources and direct attention away from rights and what goes on in courts. Yet whether one supports the court-based perspective of professional mediators or the community-based perspective of lay citizens engaged in civic work, both strains of this reform abandon an important political resource that structures bargaining in informal settings. By turning to diversion or an alternative justice system, we move away from rights as a politics resource to the politics of consensus building outside or in the shadow of legal institutions.

Appendix A
Case-Processing Time for NJC Referrals and Court Cases

	NJC	Court Cases
Two weeks or less	63% (147)	11% (57)
Three weeks	16% (38)	14% (77)
One month	12% (29)	24% (128)
Two months	8% (19)	32% (175)
Three months	1% (3)	9% (46)
Four months		2% (13)
Five months		1% (4)
Six or more months		7% (40)
Total	100% (236)	100% (540)[a]

[a]5 cases are missing data

Appendix B

Pre– and Post–NJC-Related Party Cases Referred to Court by the Prosecutor

	Type of Dispute						
	Assault	Disorder	Trespass	Vandalism	Larceny	Other	Total
Pre–NJC (1977)	58%(178)	11.4%(35)	9.1%(28)	16.6%(51)	2.3%(7)	2.6%(8)	100%(307)
Post–NJC (1978)	52%(125)	17%(40)	11%(26)	14%(34)	3%(6)	3%(7)	100%(238)

Bibliography

Aaronson, David, Bert H. Hoffa, Peter Saszi, Nicholas N. Kittrie, and David Saari (1977). *The New Justice: Alternatives to Conventional Criminal Adjudication*. Washington, D.C.: Institute for Advanced Studies in Justice, American University.

Abel, Richard L. (1979). "Delegalization: A Critical Review of Its Ideology, Manifestations, and Social Consequences," in E. Blankenburg, E. Klausa, and H. Rottleuther, eds. *Alternative Rechtsformen und Alternative zum Recht*. Bonn: Westdeutscher Verlag.

———— (1981). "Conservative Conflict and the Reproduction of Capitalism: The Role of Informal Justice." 9 *International Journal of the Sociology of Law* 245.

———— ed. (1982). *The Politics of Informal Justice*. vols. 1 and 2. New York: Academic Press.

Ad Hoc Panel on Dispute Resolution and Public Policy (1983). *Paths to Justice*. Washington, D.C.: U.S. Department of Justice and the National Institute for Dispute Resolution.

Alfini, James J., and Rachel N. Doan (1977). "A New Perspective on Misdemeanor Justice." 60 *Judicature* 425.

American Arbitration Association (1978). "Kansas City Neighborhood Justice Center Mediator Training Report." New York: American Arbitration Association.

American Bar Association (1909). "Report of the Special Committee to Suggest Remedies and Formulate Proposed Laws to Prevent Delay and Unnecessary Cost in Litigation." 34 *American Bar Association Journal* 578.

American Judicature Society and The Institute for Court Management (1978). *Misdemeanor Court Management Research Program.* Washington, D.C.: LEAA.

Amy, Douglas J. (1983). "The Politics of Environmental Mediation." 11 *Ecology Law Quarterly* 1.

Arps, Vivian, Maurice Macey, and Michael L. Thompson (1978). "The Kansas City Neighborhood Justice Center: An Alternative for Dispute Resolution." 1978 *Pretrial Services Annual Report* 1.

Ashman, Allen, and Jeffrey A. Parness (1974). "The Concept of a Unified Court System." 24 *DePaul Law Review* 1.

Auerbach, Jerold S. (1976). *Unequal Justice.* New York: Oxford University Press.

—— (1983). *Justice Without Law?.* New York: Oxford University Press.

Aumann, F. R. (1931). "Domestic Relations Courts in Ohio." 15 *Journal of the American Judicature Society* 89.

Austin, James F. (1977). "From Theory to Social Policy: Implementing Diversion Within the Criminal Justice System." Unpublished manuscript, University of California, Davis.

Baldwin, William H. (1913). "The Court of Domestic Relations of Chicago." 3 *Journal of Criminal Law, Criminology and Police Science* 400.

Baritz, Loren (1960). *The Servants of Power.* Middletown, CT: Wesleyan University Press.

Barton, John (1975). "Behind the Legal Explosion." 27 *Stanford Law Review* 567.

Baum, Lawrence, Joel Grossman, and Austin Sarat (1976). "Litigation and the Structure of Court Systems: The Role of the Political Regime in Regulating the Consumption of Court Services." Presented at the meetings of the International Political Science Association, Edinburgh, 1976.

Bell, Griffin (1977). "Testimony Before the H. R. Judiciary Committee, State of the Judiciary and Access to Justice." 95th Congress, 1st Session, June 1977.

Berkson, Larry, and Susan Carbon (1978). *Court Unification: History Politics and Implementation.* Washington, D.C.: U.S. Government Printing Office.

Best, Arthur, and Alan R. Andreasen (1977). "Consumer Response to

Unsatisfactory Purchases: A Survey of Perceiving Defects, Voicing Complaints, and Obtaining Redress." 11 *Law & Society Review* 701.

Black, Donald (1973). "The Mobilization of Law." 2 *Journal of Legal Studies* 125.

Blackburn, Abraham (1935). *The Administration of Criminal Justice in Franklin Co., Ohio.* Baltimore: Johns Hopkins Press.

Blumberg, Abraham (1967). *Criminal Justice.* Chicago: Quadrangle Books.

Blumrosen, Alfred W. (1972). "Civil Rights Conflicts: The Uneasy Search for Peace in Our Time." 1972 *Arbitration Journal* 35.

Boston, Charles A. (1917). "Some Observations Upon the Report of the Committee of the Phi Delta Phi with Special Reference to the Typical Judiciary Article for the Constitution." 73 *Annals of the American Academy of Political and Social Science* 104.

Brakel, Samuel (1971). "Informal Discretion, Motivation, and Formalization." 48 *Denver Law Journal* 211.

Braverman, Harry (1974). *Labor and Monopoly Capital.* New York: Monthly Review Press.

Breckenridge, Sophonisba (1934). *Social Work and the Courts.* Chicago: University of Chicago Press.

Brigham, John (1984). *Civil Liberties & American Democracy.* Washington, D.C.: Congressional Quarterly Press.

Brigham, John, and Don W. Brown (1980). "Introduction," in J. Brigham and D. W. Brown, eds., *Policy Implementation: Penalties or Incentives?.* Beverly Hills, CA: Sage Publications.

Bryant, Louise Stevens (1918). "A Department of Diagnosis and Treatment for the Municipal." 9 *Journal of Criminal Law and Criminology* 198.

Buckle, Leonard G., and Suzann R. Thomas-Buckle (1981). "Self-Help Justice: Dispute Processing in Urban American Neighborhoods." Presented at the annual meeting of the Law and Society Association, Amherst, 1981.

Burawoy, Michael (1979). "Towards a Marxist Theory of the Labor Process: Braverman and Beyond." 8 *Politics and Society* 247.

Burger, Warren E. (1976). "Agenda for 2000 A.D.—A Need for Systematic Anticipation." 70 *Federal Rules Decision* 83.

Cain, Maureen (1983). "Where Are the Disputes? A Study of a First Instance Civil Court in the U.K.," in M. Cain and K. Kulcsar, eds. *Disputes and the Law.* Budapest: Akademiai Kiado.

Cain, Maureen, and Kalman Kulcsar (1982). "Thinking Disputes: An

Essay on the Origins of the Dispute Industry." 16 *Law & Society Review* 381.

Cappelletti, Mauro, and Bryant Garth (1978). "Access to Justice: The Newest Wave in the World-Wide Movement to Make Rights Effective." 27 *Buffalo Law Review* 181.

Cavanagh, Ralph and Austin Sarat (1980). "Thinking About Courts: Toward and Beyond a Jurisprudence of Judicial Competence." 14 *Law & Society Review* 371.

Chandler, Alfred D. (1962). *Strategy and Structure*. Cambridge, MA: MIT Press.

Christie, Nils (1977). "Conflicts as Property." 17 *The British Journal of Criminology* 1.

Clawson, Dan (1980). *Bureaucracy in the Labor Process*. New York: Monthly Review Press.

Coates, Dan, and Stephen Penrod (1981). "Social Psychology and Emergence of Disputes." 15 *Law & Society Review* 655.

Cohen, Julius Henry (1917). "Administration of Business and Discipline by the Courts." 73 *Annals of American Academy of Political and Social Science* 205.

Columbia Law Review (1934). "Small Claims Courts." 34 *Columbia Law Review* 932.

Conner, Ross F., and Ray Surette (1977). *The Citizen Dispute Settlement Program: Resolving Disputes Outside the Courts—Orlando, Florida*. Chicago: American Bar Association.

Connick, E., J. Chytilo, and A. Person (1980). "Battered Women and the New York City Criminal Justice System." Presented at the annual meeting of the Law and Society Association and the International Sociological Association, Madison, 1980.

Cook, Royce F., Janice A. Roehl, and David I. Sheppard (1980). *Neighborhood Justice Centers Field Test: Final Evaluation Report*. Washington, D.C.: U.S. Department of Justice.

Cotterrell, Roger (1983a). "Legality and Political Legitimacy in the Sociology of Max Weber," in D. Sugarman, ed. *Legality, Ideology and the State*. London: Academic Press.

———— (1983b). "The Sociology Concept of Law." 10 *Journal of Law and Society* 241.

Cover, Robert M. (1979). "Dispute Resolution: A Forward." 88 *Yale Law Journal* 911.

Cratsley, John (1978). "Community Courts: Offering Alternative Dispute Resolution Within the Judicial System." 3 *Vermont Law Review* 1.

D'Alemberte, Talbot D., and Earl F. Johnson (1979). "Testimony Before the H. R. Subcommittee on Courts, Civil Liberties, and the Administration of Justice, Committee on the Judiciary and Subcommittee on Consumer Protection and Finance, Committee on Interstate and Foreign Commerce." 96th Congress, 1st Session, June 1979.

Danzig, Richard (1973). "Toward the Creation of a Complementary, Decentralized System of Criminal Justice." 26 *Stanford Law Review* 1.

Danzig, Richard and Michael Lowy (1975). "Everyday Disputes and Mediation in the U.S.: A Reply to Professor Felstiner." 9 *Law & Society Review* 675.

Davis, Kenneth Culp (1969). *Discretionary Justice.* Baton Rouge: Louisiana State University Press.

Davis, Robert C., Martha Tichane, and Deborah Grayson (1980). *Mediation and Arbitration as Alternatives to Prosecution in Felony Arrest Cases: An Evaluation of the Brooklyn Dispute Resolution Center.* New York: Vera Institute of Justice.

Day, C. B. (1928). "The Development of the Family Court." 136 *The Annals of the American Academy of Political and Social Science* 105.

Dellapa, Fred (1977). "Citizen Dispute Settlement: A New Look at an Old Method." 51 *The Florida Bar Journal* 516.

Dispute Resolution Act (1980). Public Law 96–190, February 12, 1980, 96th Congress.

Dolbeare, Kenneth (1967). *Trial Courts in Urban Politics.* New York: John Wiley & Sons.

Donzelot, Jacques (1979). *The Policing of Families.* New York: Pantheon Books.

Douglass, Paul F. (1932). *The Justice of the Peace Courts of Hamilton County, Ohio.* Baltimore: Johns Hopkins Press.

Downie, Leonard (1971). *Justice Denied: The Case for Reform in the Courts.* Baltimore: Penguin Books, Inc.

Edelman, Murray (1977). *Political Language: Words that Succeed and Policies that Fail.* New York: Academic Press.

Edholm, Charlton Lawrence (1915). "The Small Debtors Court." 22 *Case and Comment* 29.

Edwards, Richard (1979). *Contested Terrain.* New York: Basic Books.

Ehrlich, Thomas (1977). "Testimony Before the H. R. Judiciary Committee, State of the Judiciary and Access to Justice." 95th Congress, 1st Session, June 1977.

——— (1978). Letter to Robert Kastenmeier, Chairman, November 9, 1978, Subcommittee on Courts, Civil Liberties, and the Administration of Justice, Committee on the Judiciary, Hearing Before the Subcommittee, July 27, August 2, 1978.

Eisenberg, Melvin A. (1976). "Private Ordering Through Negotiation: Dispute Settlement and Rule-Making." 89 *Harvard Law Review* 635.

Eisenstein, James, and Herbert Jacob (1977). *Felony Justice.* Boston: Little, Brown.

Elliott, Sheldon D. (1959). *Improving Our Courts.* New York: Oceana Publications.

Ellis, Richard E. (1971). *The Jeffersonian Crisis.* New York: Oxford University Press.

Engel, David (1980). "Legal Pluralism in an American Community: Perspectives on a Civil Trial Court." 3 *American Bar Foundation Research Journal* 425.

Faust, Frederick L., and Paul J. Brantingham, eds. (1974). *Juvenile Justice Philosophy.* St. Paul, MN: West Publishing Co.

Feeley, Malcolm M. (1973). "Two Models of the Criminal Justice System: An Organizational Perspective." 7 *Law & Society Review* 407.

———— (1976). "The Concept of Laws in Social Science: A Critique and Notes on an Expanded View." 10 *Law & Society Review* 497.

———— (1979). *The Process is the Punishment.* New York: Russell Sage.

———— (1983). *Court Reform on Trial.* New York: Basic Books.

Felstiner, William L. F. (1974). "Influences of Social Organization on Dispute Processing." 9 *Law & Society Review* 63.

———— (1975). "Avoidance as Dispute Processing: An Elaboration." 9 *Law & Society Review* 695.

Felstiner, William L. F., and Lynne Williams (1979). "Mediation as an Alternative to Criminal Prosecution." 2 *Law and Human Behavior* 233.

———— (1980). *Community Mediation in Dorchester, Massachusetts.* Washington, D.C.: U.S. Department of Justice.

Felstiner, William L. F., Richard L. Abel, and Austin Sarat (1981). "The Emergence and Transformation of Disputes: Naming, Blaming, Claiming." 15 *Law & Society Review* 631.

Fisher, Eric A. (1975). "Community Courts: An Alternative to Conventional Criminal Adjudication." 24 *The American University Law Review* 1253.

Fitzgerald, Jeffrey, and Richard Dickins (1981). "Disputing in Legal and Nonlegal Contexts: Some Questions for Sociologists of Law."

15 *Law & Society Review* 681.

Fitzpatrick, Peter (1983). "Law, Plurality and Underdevelopment," in D. Sugarman, ed., *Legality, Ideology and the State.* London: Academic Press.

Florida Supreme Court, Office of the State Courts Administrator, Dispute Resolution Alternatives Committee (1979). *The Citizen Dispute Settlement Process in Florida.* Judicial Planning and Coordination Unit.

Ford Foundation (1978a). *Mediating Social Conflict.* New York: Ford Foundation.

——— (1978b). *New Approaches to Conflict Resolution.* New York: Ford Foundation.

Foucault, Michel (1977). *Discipline and Punishment: The Birth of the Prison.* New York: Pantheon.

Fox, Sanford J. (1970). "Juvenile Justice Reform: An Historical Perspective." 22 *Stanford Law Review* 1187.

Friedman, Lawrence (1984). *Legislation on Dispute Resolution.* Washington, D.C.: American Bar Association.

Friedman, Lawrence, and Robert Percival (1981). *The Roots of Justice: Crime and Punishment in Alameda County, California, 1870–1910.* Chapel Hill, NC: University of North Carolina Press.

Fuller, Lon L. (1963). "Collective Bargaining and the Arbitrator." 1963 *Wisconsin Law Review* 3.

——— (1971). "Mediation—Its Forms and Functions." 44 *Southern California Law Review* 305.

——— (1978). "The Forms and Limits of Adjudication." 92 *Harvard Law Review* 353.

Galanter, Marc (1974). "Why the 'Haves' Come Out Ahead: Speculations on the Limits of Legal Change." 9 *Law & Society Review* 95.

——— (1976a). "Delivering Legality: Some Proposals for the Direction of Research." 11 *Law & Society Review* 225.

——— (1976b). "The Duty Not to Deliver Legal Services." 30 *University of Miami Law Review* 929.

——— (1979). "Legality and Its Discontents: A Preliminary Assessment of Current Theories of Legalization and Delegalization," in E. Blankenburg, E. Klausa, and H. Rottleuthuer, eds., *Alternative Rechtsformen und Alternative zum Recht.* Bonn: Westdeutscher Verlag.

———— (1981). "Justice in Many Rooms." 19 *Journal of Legal Plural-ism and Unofficial Law* 1.

———— (1983). "Reading the Landscape of Disputes: What We Know and Don't Know (and Think We Know) About Our Allegedly Contentious and Litigious Society." 31 *UCLA Law Review* 4.

Gallas, Geoff (1976). "The Conventional Wisdom of State Court Administration: A Critical Assessment and an Alternative Approach." 2 *Justice System Journal* 35.

Galub, Arthur L. (1968). "The Politics of Court Reorganization in New York State." Unpublished Ph.D. dissertation, Department of Political Science, Columbia University.

Garth, Bryant (1982). "The Movement Toward Procedural Informalism in North America and Western Europe: A Critical Survey," in R. L. Abel, ed. *The Politics of Internal Justice*, vol. 2: *The Comparative Experience*. New York: Academic Press.

Gazell, James A. (1977). "The Principal Facets and Goals of Court Management: A Sketch," in L. Berkson, S. Hays, and S. Carbon, eds., *Managing the State Courts*. St. Paul, MN: West Publishing Co.

Gilbert, Hiram (1928). *The Municipal Court of Chicago*. Chicago: Author.

Glazer, Nathan (1975). "Towards an Imperial Judiciary?" 41 *The Public Interest* 104.

Goldstein, Burton B. (1976). "Due Process in Public Schools." 1976 *North Carolina Law Review*.

Goldstein, Herman (1977). *Policing a Free Society*. Cambridge, MA: Ballinger Publishing Co.

Gordon, Robert (1984). "Critical Legal Histories." 36 *Stanford Law Review* 57.

Gorelick, Jamie S. (1975). "Pretrial Diversion: The Threat of Expanding Social Control." 10 *Harvard Civil Rights–Civil Liberties Law Review* 180.

Gottheil, Diane L. (1979). "Pretrial Diversion: A Response to the Critics." 25 *Crime and Delinquency* 65.

Green, Mark (1978). "Testimony Before the H. R. Subcommittee on Courts, Civil Liberties, and the Administration of Justice of the Committee on the Judiciary." 95th Congress 2nd Session, July 1978.

Greene, J. Kent (1910). "The Municipal Court of Chicago," 58 *University of Pennsylvania Law Review* 335.

Grevstad, Nicolay (1918). "Norway's Conciliation Tribunal." 2 *Journal of the American Judicature Society* 5.

Griffith, John (1969). "Ideology in Criminal Procedure or a Third 'Model' of the Criminal Process." 79 *Yale Law Journal* 359.

Grossman, Joel, and Austin Sarat (1975). "Litigation in the Federal Courts: A Comparative Perspective." 9 *Law & Society Review* 346.

—— (1981). "Access to Justice and the Limits of Law." 3 *Law & Policy* 125.

Grossman, Joel, Austin Sarat, Herbert Kritzer, Stephen McDougal, Kristin Bumillers, and Richard Miller (1982). "Dimensions of Institutional Participation: Who Uses the Courts and How? 44 *The Journal of Politics* 86.

Gulver, P. H. (1973). "Negotiation as a Mode of Dispute Settlement." 7 *Law & Society Review* 667.

Gusfield, Joseph R. (1972). *Symbolic Crusade*. Urbana: University of Illinois Press.

Gutek, Barbara A. (1978). "Strategies for Studying Client Satisfaction." 34 *Journal of Social Issues* 44.

Habermas, Jurgen (1973). *Legitimation Crisis*. Boston: Beacon Press.

Hall, Stuart, Chas Critcher, Tony Jefferson, John Clark, and Brian Roberts (1978). *Policing the Crisis*. London: MacMillan Press.

Haller, Mark H. (1976). "Historical Roots of Police Behavior: Chicago, 1880–1925." 10 *Law & Society Review* 303.

Halliday, Terence Charles (1979). *Parameters of Professional Influence Policies and Politics of the Chicago Bar Association, 1945–70*, Unpublished Ph.D. dissertation, Department of Sociology, University of Chicago.

Halpern, Stephen (1978). "An Imperial Judiciary: Notes on Comparative Institutional Development and Power in America." Presented at the annual meetings of the American Political Science Association, New York, 1978.

Handler, Joel (1966). "Controlling Official Behavior in Welfare Administration." 54 *California Law Review*.

—— (1978). *Social Movements and the Legal System*. New York: Academic Press.

Harley, Herbert (1912a). "A Circular Letter Concerning the Administration of Justice." Chicago: American Judicature Society Archives.

—— (1912b). "The Scientific Attitude Toward Reform in Procedure." 75 *Central Law Journal* 147.

—— (1915a). "Court Organization for a Metropolitan District." 9 *American Political Science Review* 507.

—— (1915b). "The Small Claims Branch of the Municipal Court Chicago." *American Judicature Society* (Bulletin No. 8).

—— (1915c). "Ultimate Types of Interior Courts and Judges." 22 *Case and Comment* 3.

—— (1917a). "An Efficient County Court System." 73 *Annals of the American Academy of Political and Social Science* 189.

—— (1917b). "Business Management for the Courts." 5 *Virginia Law Review* 1.

—— (1926). "Conciliation Procedure in Small Claims." 125 *Annals of the American Academy of Political and Social Science* 91.

Hartmann, Edward G. (1948). *The Movement to Americanize the Immigrant*. New York: Columbia University Press.

Hartogensis, B. H. (1929). "A Successful Community Court." 12 *Journal of the American Judicature Society* 183.

Harvard Law Review (1976). "Comment." *Harvard Law Review*.

Hay, Douglas, Peter Linebaugh, John G. Rule, E. P. Thompson, and Cal Winslow (1975). *Albion's Fatal Tree: Crime and Society in Eighteenth-Century England*. New York: Pantheon.

Hays, Samuel (1964). "Municipal Reform in the Progressive Era: Whose Class Interest?" 55 *Pacific Northwest Quarterly* 157.

Hays, Steven (1977). "Contemporary Trends in Court Unification," in L. Berkson, S. Hays, and S. Carbon, eds., *Managing the State Courts*. St. Paul, MN: West Publishing Co.

Henderson, Thomas A., and Cornelius M. Kerwin (1982). "The Changing Character of Court Organization." 7 *The Justice System Journal* 449.

Heydebrand, Wolf (1979). "The Technocratic Administration of Justice." 2 *Research in Law and Sociology* 29.

—— (1983a). "Technocratic Administration: Beyond Weber's Bureaucracy." Unpublished manuscript, Sociology Department, New York University.

—— (1983b). "Technocratic Corporatism: Toward a Theory of Occupational and Organization Transformation," in R. H. Hall, and R. E. Quinn, eds., *Organizational Theory and Public Policy*. Beverly Hills, CA: Sage Publications.

Heydebrand, Wolf, and Carroll Seron (1981). "The Double Bind of the Capitalist Judicial System." 9 *International Journal of the Sociology of Law* 407.

Hirschhorn, Larry (1978). "The Political Economy of Social Service Rationalization: A Developmental View." 2 *Contemporary Crises* 63.

Hirst, Paul (1979). *On Law and Ideology*. Atlantic Highlands, NJ: Humanities Press.

Hofrichter, Richard (1977). "Justice Centers Raise Basic Questions." 2 *New Directions in Legal Services* 168.

───── (1982). "Neighborhood Justice and the Social Control Problems of American Capitalism: A Perspective," in R. Abel, ed., *The Politics of Informal Justice*, vol. 1: *The American Experience*. New York: Academic Press.

Hofstadter, Richard (1955). *The Age of Reform*. New York: Knopf.

Horowitz, Donald L. (1977). *The Courts and Social Policy*. Washington, D.C.: Brookings Institution.

Horwitz, Morton J. (1977). *The Transformation of American Law 1789–1860*. Cambridge, MA: Harvard University Press.

Howard, T. L. (1935). "The Justice of the Peace System in Tennessee." 13 *Tennessee Law Review* 19.

Hunt, Alan (1978). *The Sociological Movement in Law*. London: MacMillan Press.

───── (1985). "The Ideology of Law: Advances and Problems in Recent Applications of the Concept of Ideology to the Analysis of Law." 19 *Law & Society Review* 11.

Hurst, James Willard (1953). "Changing Popular Views About Law and Lawyers." 287 *The Annals of the American Academy of Political and Social Science* 1.

───── (1956). *Law and the Conditions of Freedom*. Madison, WI: University of Wisconsin Press.

Ireland, Robert M. (1972). *The County Courts in Antebellum Kentucky*. Lexington, KY: University Press of Kentucky.

Jacob, Herbert (1973). *Urban Justice: Law and Order in American Cities*. Englewood Cliffs, NJ: Prentice-Hall, Inc.

───── (1983). "Understanding How Courts Do Their Work," in K. Boyum, and L. Mather, eds., *Empirical Theories About Courts*. New York: Longman.

Jacoby, A. L. (1923). "The Psychopathic Clinic in the Criminal Court: Its Uses and Possibilities." 7 *Journal of the American Judicature Society* 21.

Jessup, Henry W. (1917). "The Simplification of the Machinery of Justice with a View to Its Greater Efficiency." 73 *Annals of the American Academy of Political and Social Science* 1.

Johnson, Earl (1977). "Let the Tribunal Fit the Case—Establishing Criteria for Channeling Matters into Dispute Resolution Mechanisms." 80 *Federal Rules Decisions*.

───── (1978). *Courts and the Community*. Williamsburg, VA: National Center for State Courts.

Johnson, Earl, Valerie Kantor, Elizabeth Schwartz (1977). *Outside the Courts: A Survey of Diversion Alternatives in Civil Cases*. Williamsburg, VA: National Center for State Courts.

Journal of the American Judicature Society (JAJS) (1918a). "Commercial Arbitration." 2 *Journal of the American Judicature Society* 156.

—— (1918b). "Informal Procedure in Chicago." 2 *Journal of the American Judicature Society* 23.

—— (1918c). "Informal Procedure in New York." 2 *Journal of the American Judicature Society* 26.

—— (1919a). "Act to Provide for Conciliation." 2 *Journal of the American Judicature Society* 151.

—— (1919b). "Unnecessary Litigation." 2 *Journal of the American Judicature Society* 158.

—— (1922a). "Arbitration Society of America." 6 *Journal of the American Judicature Society* 59.

—— (1922b). "Conciliation Law Held Valid." 6 *Journal of the American Judicature Society* 133.

—— (1923). "Try Conciliation in Iowa." 7 *Journal of the American Judicature Society* 15.

—— (1928). "Great City Court Given Management." 12 *Journal of the American Judicature Society* 116.

Judicial Conference of the ABA (1976). *Pound Conference.* "The Causes of Popular Dissatisfaction of the Administration of Justice." 70 *Federal Rules Decision.*

Kastenmeier, Robert (1979). "Dispute Resolution Act Report." Committee on the Judiciary, H. R. 96th Congress, 1st Session, October 23, 1979.

Keating, Michael (1975). "Arbitration of Inmate Grievances." 30 *Arbitration Journal* 177.

Keebler, Robert S. (1930). "Our Justice of the Peace Courts—A Problem in Justice." 9 *Tennessee Law Review* 1.

Kellor, Frances (1914). "Justice for the Immigrant." 52 *Annals of the American Academy of Political and Social Science* 159.

Kennedy, Duncan (1973). "Legal Formality." 2 *The Journal of Legal Studies* 351.

—— (1979). "The Structure of Blackstone's Commentaries." 28 *Buffalo Law Review* 205.

Kidder, Robert (1981). "The End of the Road?: Problems in Analysis of Disputes." 15 *Law & Society Review* 717.

Kirp, David (1976). "Proceduralism and Bureaucracy: Due Process in the School Setting." 28 *Stanford Law Review.*

Klare, Karl (1979). "Law Making as Praxis." 40 *Telos* 123.

Kogan, Herman (1974). *The First Century: The Chicago Bar Association 1874–1974.* New York: Rand McNally and Co.

Larson, Magali Sarfatti (1977). *The Rise of Professionalism.* Berkeley, CA: University of California Press.

Lasch, Christopher (1965). *The New Radicalism of America 1889–1963.* New York: Knopf.

Lauer, Edgar J. (1918). "Conciliation and Arbitration in the Municipal Court of the City of New York." 1 *Journal of the American Judicature Society* 153.

——— (1928). "Conciliation—A Cure for the Law's Delay." 136 *Annals of the American Academy for Political and Social Science* 54.

——— (1929). "Conciliation: A Cure for Congested Court Calendars." 27 *New York Legal Aid Review* 1.

Law Enforcement Assistance Administration (LEAA) (1974). *Citizens Dispute Settlement: The Night Prosecutor Program of Columbus, Ohio.* Washington, D.C.: U.S. Department of Justice.

——— (1979). "Justice Centers Ease Caseload." 8 *LEAA Newsletter* 1.

Lempert, Richard O. (1976). "Mobilizing Private Law." 11 *Law & Society Review* 173.

Levin, Martin A. (1977). *Urban Politics and the Criminal Courts.* Chicago: University of Chicago Press.

Levine, Manuel (1915). "The Conciliation Court of Cleveland." *American Judicature Society Bulletin* 8.

Lieberman, Jethro K., ed., (1984). *The Role of Courts in American Society.* The Final Report of the Council on the Role of Courts. St. Paul, MN: West Publishing Co.

Lipsky, Michael (1980). *Street-Level Bureaucracy.* New York: Russell Sage Foundation.

Lufler, Henry, Michael Roth, and Jonathan Becker (1976). "The *Goss* Case and School Discipline Procedure in Search of Substance." Madison WI: Center for Public Representation.

Lupe, John J. (1928). "Domestic Relations Branch." 1928 *Annual Reports of the Municipal Court of Chicago* 101.

Lustig, R. Jeffrey (1982). *Corporate Liberalism: The Origins of Modern American Political Theory, 1890–1920.* Berkeley, CA: University of California Press.

Macaulay, Stewart (1963). "Non-Contractual Relations in Business: A Preliminary Study." 28 *American Sociological Review* 55.

Maguire, John MacArthur (1926). "The Model Poor Litigants' Statute." 125 *Annals of the American Academy of Political and Social Science* 84.

Mann, Bruce (1980). "Rationality, Legal Change, and Community in Connecticut, 1690–1760." 14 *Law & Society Review* 187.

—— (1984). "The Formalization of Informal Law: Arbitration Before the American Revolution." 59 *New York University Law Review*.

Mannel, Robert M. (1973). *Thorns & Thistles: Juvenile Delinquents in the U. S., 1825–1940*. Hanover, NH: University Press of New England.

Martin, Del (1976). *Battered Wives*. New York: Pocket Books.

Mather, Lynn, and Barbara Yngvesson (1981). "Language, Audience, and the Transformation of Disputes." 15 *Law & Society Review* 775.

Mayhew, Leon H. (1975). "Institutions of Representation: Civil Justice and the Public." 9 *Law & Society Review* 401.

McBarnet, Doreen (1981). "Magistrates' Courts and the Ideology of Justice." 8 *British Journal of Law and Society* 181.

McEwen, Craig, and Richard J. Maiman (1984). "Mediation in Small Claims Court: Achieving Compliance Through Consent." 18 *Law & Society Review* 11.

McGillis, Daniel (1980). "Recent Developments in Minor Dispute Processing." Cambridge, MA: Center for Criminal Justice, Harvard Law School.

McGillis, Daniel, and Joan Mullen (1977). *Neighborhood Justice Centers: An Analysis of Potential Models*. Washington, D.C.: LEAA.

McKean, Dayton D. (1963). *The Integrated Bar*. Boston: Houghton Mifflin Co.

Meador, Daniel (1978). "Testimony Before the H.R. Subcommittee on Consumer Protection and Finance of the Committee on Interstate and Foreign Commerce." 95th Congress, 2nd Session, July 20, and 21, 1978.

Merry, Sally Engle (1979). "Going to Court: Strategies of Dispute Management in an American Urban Neighborhood." 13 *Law & Society Review* 891.

——(1982). "The Social Organization of Mediation in Nonindustrial Societies: Implications for Informal Community Justice in America," in R. L. Abel ed. *The Politics of Informal Justice*, vol 2: *The Comparative Experience*. New York: Academic Press.

—— (1985). "Concepts of Law and Justice Among Working Class Americans: Ideology as Culture." 9 *Legal Studies Forum* 59.

Merry, Sally Engle, and Susan Silbey (forthcoming). "Mediator Ideology and Settlement Strategies. *Law & Policy.*

Meyer, J., and T. Lorimor (1977). "Police Intervention Data and Domestic Violence." Report prepared for the National Institute on
Mental Health.

Mileski, Maureen (1971). "Courtroom Encounters: An Observation
Study of Lower Criminal Courts." 5 *Law & Society Review* 473.

Miller, Richard E., and Austin Sarat (1981). "Grievances, Claims, and
Disputes: Assessing the Adversary Culture." 15 *Law & Society
Review* 525.

Mnookin, Robert H., and Lewis Kornhauser (1979). "Bargaining in
the Shadow of the Law: The Case of Divorce." 88 *Yale Law
Journal* 950.

Moss-Magnuson Warranty Act, 1975.

Munger, Frank (1982). "Movements for Court Reform: A Preliminary
Interpretation," in P. Dubois, ed. *The Politics of Judicial Reform.* Lexington, MA: Lexington Press.

Munger, Frank, and Carroll Seron (1984). "Critical Legal Studies
versus Critical Legal Theory: A Comment on Method." 6 *Law
& Policy* 257.

Myers, Martha A., and John Hagan (1979). "Private and Public Trouble: Prosecutors and the Allocation of Court Resources." 26 *Social Problems* 439.

Nader, Laura (1979). "Disputing Without the Force of Law." 88 *Yale
Law Journal* 998.

Nader, Laura, and Linda Singer (1976). "Dispute Resolution in the
Future: What are the Choices?" 51 *California State Bar Journal* 281.

Nader, Laura, and Harry Todd, eds., (1978). *The Disputing Process—
Law in Ten Societies.* New York: Columbia University Press.

National Advisory Commission on Criminal Justice Standards and
Goals—Task Force on Courts (1973). *Commission Report.*
Washington, D.C.: Government Printing Office.

National Center on Women & Family Law (1984). "Report on the
Conference on Women and Mediation." New York University
School of Law, New York, January, 1984.

National Institute for Dispute Resolution (1984). *Dispute Resolution
Resource Directory.* Washington, D.C.: National Institute for
Dispute Resolution.

Nehemkis, Peter R. Jr. (1933). "The Boston Poor Debtor Court—A
Study in Collection Procedure." 42 *Yale Law Journal* 561.

Nejelski, Paul (1976). "Diversion: The Promise and the Danger." 22 *Crime and Delinquency* 93.

New York Law Review (1925). "Do Litigants Want Law and Not Conciliation?" 3 *New York Law Review* 425.

Nicolau, George, and Gerald W. Cormick (1972). "Community Disputes and the Resolution of Conflict: Another View." 27 *Arbitration Journal*.

Nimmer, Raymond (1974). *Diversion: The Search for Alternative Forms of Prosecution.* Chicago: American Bar Foundation.

Nonet, Philippe, and Philip Selznick (1978). *Law and Society in Transition: Toward Responsive.* New York: Harper.

O'Connor, James (1973). *The Fiscal Crisis of the State.* New York: St. Martin's.

Offe, Claus (1974). "Structural Problems of the Capitalist State," in Von Beyme, ed., *German Political Studies*, Vol. 1, Los Angeles.

——— (1975). "The Theory of the Capitalist State and the Problem of Policy Formation," in L. Lindberg and C. Offe, eds. *Stress and Contradiction in Modern Capital.* Lexington, MA: Lexington Books.

Offe, Claus, and Volker Ronge (1975). "Theses on the Theory of the State." *New German Critique* 137.

Packer, Herbert (1968). *The Limits of the Criminal Sanction.* Stanford, CA: Stanford University Press.

Paddon, Mary E. (1920). "The Inferior Criminal Courts of New York City." 11 *Journal of Criminal Law, Criminology and Police Science* 8.

Parnas, Raymond (1970). "Judicial Response to Intra-Family Violence." 54 *Minnesota Law Review* 585.

Pearson, Jessica (1982). "An Evaluation of Alternatives to Court Adjudication." 7 *The Justice System Journal* 420.

Pipkin, Ronald M., and Janet Rifkin (1984). "The Social Organization in Alternative Dispute Resolution: Implications for Professionalization of Mediation." 9 *Justice System Journal* 204.

Platt, Anthony (1969). *The Child Savers.* Chicago: University of Chicago Press.

Potter, William (1922). "Give Judiciary Greater Power." 6 *Journal of the American Judicature Society* 164.

Pound, Roscoe (1906). "The Causes of Popular Dissatisfaction with the Administration of Justice." 29 *American Bar Association Reports* 395.

——— (1912). "Social Problems and the Courts." 18 *American Journal of Sociology* 331.

—— (1913). "The Administration of Justice in the Modern City." 26 *Harvard Law Review* 302.

—— (1940a). *Organization of Courts.* Boston: Little, Brown.

—— (1940b). "Principles and Outline of a Modern Unified Court Organization." 23 *Journal of the American Judicature Society* 225.

Ransom, William L. (1917a). "The Layman's Demand for Improved Judicial Machinery." 73 *Annals of the American Academy of Political and Social Science* 132.

—— (1917b). "The Organization of the Courts for the Better Administration of Justice." 2 *Cornell Law Quarterly* 261.

Ray, Larry (1981). *Dispute Resolution Program Directory.* Washington, D.C.: American Bar Association.

—— (1983). *Dispute Resolution Program Directory.* Washington, D.C.: American Bar Association.

Reich, Charles (1964). "The New Property." 73 *Yale Law Journal.*

—— (1965). "Individual Rights and Social Welfare: The Emerging Legal Issues." 74 *Yale Law Journal.*

—— (1966). "Social Welfare in Public-Private State." 1966 *University of Pennsylvania Law Review.*

Rheinstein, Max, ed. (1925). *Max Weber and Law in Economy and Society.* New York: Simon and Schuster.

Richardson, Lee (1978). "Testimony Before the H.R. Subcommittee on Consumer Protection and Finance of the Committee on Interstate and Foreign Commerce." 95th Congress, 2nd Session, July 20 and 21, 1978.

Rifkind, Simon (1976). "Are We Asking Too Much of Our Courts?" 70 *Federal Rules Decisions* 96.

Robbins, A. H. (1916). "Preventing Unnecessary Litigation at the Source." 82 *Central Law Journal* 280.

Roberts, Peter (1920). *The Problem of Americanization.* New York: Macmillan.

Robertson, John A. (1972). "Pre-Trial Diversion of Drug Offenders: A Statutory Approach." 52 *Boston University Law Review.*

——, ed. (1974). *Rough Justice: Perspectives in Lower Criminal Courts.* Boston: Little, Brown.

Roesch, George F. (1904). "The Municipal Court." 1 *Municipal Court Review* 4.

Roesch, Ronald (1978). "Does Adult Diversion Work?: The Failure of Research on Criminal Justice." 24 *Crime and Delinquency* 72.

Root, Elihu (1916). "Public Service by the Bar." 41 *Reports of the American Bar Association* 358.

Rosenberg, Maurice (1977). "Let the Tribunal Fit the Case: Establishing Criteria for Channeling Matters into Dispute Resolution Mechanisms." 80 *Federal Rules Decisions* 147.

—— (1981). "Civil Justice Research and Civil Justice Reform." 15 *Law & Society Review* 473.

Rosener, Judy B. (1977). "Citizen Participation: Can We Measure Its Effectiveness?" 48 *Public Administration Review* 457.

Rothman, David J. (1980). *Conscience and Convenience*. Boston: Little, Brown.

Ruhnka, J., and S. Weller (1978). *Small Claims Courts: A National Examination*. Williamsburg, VA: National Center for State Courts.

Ryan, John Paul (1981). "Adjudication and Sentencing in a Misdemeanor Court: The Outcome is the Punishment." 15 *Law & Society Review* 79.

Ryerson, Ellen (1978). *The Best-Laid Plans*. New York: Hill and Wang.

Sacks, Albert M. (1984). "Legal Education and the Changing Role of Lawyers in Dispute Resolution." 34 *Journal of Legal Education* 237.

Sander, Frank E. A. (1976). "Varieties of Dispute Processing." 70 *Federal Rules Decisions* 79.

—— (1977). *Report on the National Conference on Minor Disputes Resolution*. Chicago: American Bar Association.

—— (1984). "Alternative Dispute Resolution in the Law School Curriculum: Opportunities and Obstacles." 34 *Journal of Legal Education* 229.

Santos, Boaventura De Sousa (1979). "Popular Justice, Dual Power and Socialist Strategy," in B. Fine et al., eds., *Capitalism and the Rule of Law*. London: Hutchinson.

—— (1980). "Law and Community: The Changing Nature of State Power in Late Capitalism." 8 *International Journal of the Sociology of Law* 379.

Sarat, Austin (1976). "Alternatives in Dispute Processing: Litigation in a Small Claims Court." 10 *Law & Society Review* 339.

Sarat, Austin and Joel Grossman (1975). "Courts and Conflict Resolution: Problems in the Mobilization of Adjudication." 69 *American Political Science Review* 1199.

Scheingold, Stuart (1974). *The Politics of Rights*. New Haven: Yale University Press.

Schiesl, Martin J. (1977). *The Politics of Efficiency: Municipal Administration and Reform in America*. Berkeley, CA: University of California Press.

Schramm, Gustav L. (1928). *Piedpoure Courts: A Study of the Small Claim Litigant in the Pittsburgh District*. The Legal Aid Society of Pittsburgh, Press of Smith Bros., Co., Inc.

Schultz, J. Lawrence (1973). "The Cycle of Juvenile Court History." 17 *Crime and Delinquency* 457.

Schultz, Mark (1978). "Testimony Before the H. R. Subcommittee on Consumer Protection and Finance of the Committee on Interstate and Foreign Commerce." 95th Congress, 2nd Session, July 20 and 21, 1978.

Scott, Austin W. (1923). "Small Causes and Poor Litigants." 9 *American Bar Association Journal* 457.

Scull, Andrew T. (1977). *Decarceration: Community Treatment and the Deviant—A Radical View*. Englewood Cliffs, NJ: Prentice-Hall.

Seifert, Randolph J. (1978). Letter to the H. R. Subcommittee on Consumer Protection and Finance of the Committee on Interstate and Foreign Commerce. H. R. 95th Congress, 2nd Session, July 20 and 21, 1978.

Seron, Carroll (1978). *Judicial Reorganization*. Lexington, MA: Lexington Books.

Shapiro, Martin (1975). "Courts," in D. Greenstein and N. Polsby, eds., *Handbook of Political Science*. Reading, MA: Addison.

———— (1981). *Courts: A Comparative Perspective*. Chicago: University of Chicago Press.

Sheppard, David I., Janice A. Roehl., and Royer F. Cook (1978). *Neighborhood Justice Centers Field Test: Implementation Study*. Reston, VA: Institute for Social Analysis.

Shick, R. P. (1926). "Simplifying Criminal Procedure in the Lower Courts." 125 *The Annals of the American Academy of Political and Social Science* 112.

Shklar, Judith (1964). *Legalism*. Cambridge, MA: Harvard University Press.

Shonholtz, Raymond (1977). "Review of Alternative Dispute Mechanisms and a Government Proposal for Neighborhood Justice Centers." San Francisco: San Francisco Community Board Program.

———— (1978). "Testimony Before the Subcommittee on Courts, Civil Liberties, and the Administration of Justice, Committee on the Judiciary Dispute Resolution Act, S. 957." H.R. 95th Congress, 2nd Session, July 27 and August 2, 1978.

———— (1979). "Testimony Before the Subcommittee on Courts, Civil Liberties, and the Administration of Justice, Committee on

Judiciary and Subcommittee on Consumer Protection and Finance, Committee on Interstate and Foreign Commerce, Resolution of Minor Disputes." H.R. 96th Congress, 1st Session, June 6, 7, 14, and 18, 1979.

Silbey, Susan S. (1981). "Making Sense of the Lower Courts." 6 *Justice System Journal* 13.

——— (1984). "The Consequence of Responsive Regulation," in K. Hawkins and J. Thomas, eds. *Enforcing Regulation*. Boston: Kluwer-Nijhoff Publishing Co.

Silverstein, Lee (1955). "Small Claims Courts Versus Justice of Peace." 58 *West Virginia Law Review* 241.

Simkin, William E. (1971). *Mediation and the Dynamics of Collective Bargaining*. Washington, D.C.: Bureau of National Affairs, Inc.

Simon, William H. (1978). "The Ideology of Advocacy: Procedural Justice and Professional Ethics." 1978 *Wisconsin Law Review* 29.

Singer, Linda (1979). "The Growth of Non-Judicial Dispute Resolution: Speculations on the Effects on Justice for the Poor and on the Role of Legal Services." Washington, D.C.: Legal Service Corporation.

Skolnick, Jerome (1966). *Justice Without Trial*. New York: John Wiley & Sons.

——— (1967). "Social Control in the Adversary System." 11 *Journal of Conflict Resolution* 52.

Skowronek, Stephen (1982). *Building a New American State: The Expansion of National Administrative Capacities, 1877–1920*. New York: Cambridge University Press.

Smith, Chester H. (1927). "The Justice of the Peace System in the United States." 15 *California Law Review* 118.

Smith, Reginald Heber (1919a). "Denial of Justice." 3 *Journal of the American Judicature Society* 112.

——— (1919b). *Justice and the Poor*. New York: Charles Scribner's Sons.

——— (1924a). "Report of the Committee on Small Claims and Conciliation of the ABA." 22 *New York Legal Aid Review* 1.

——— (1924b). "Small Claims Procedure is Succeeding." 8 *Journal of the American Judicature Society* 1.

——— (1926). "Simplified Procedure in the Administration of Justice: The Danish Conciliation System." 1926 *Monthly Labor Review* 1.

——— (1928). "Conciliation and Legal Aid an Opportunity for Pioneering." 136 *Annals of American Academy of Political and Social Science* 80.

Snyder, Francis G. (1981). "Anthropology, Dispute Processes and Law: A Critical Introduction." 8 *British Journal of Law and Society* 141.

Snyder, Frederick E. (1978). "Crime and Community Mediation—The Boston Experience: A Preliminary Report on the Dorchester Urban Court Program." 3 *Wisconsin Law Review* 737.

Sonsteby, John J. (1932). *Business Methods in Courts.* Chicago: Champlin-Shealey Co.

Spitzer, Steven (1982). "The Dialectics of Formal and Informal Control," in R. Abel, ed., *The Politics of Informal Justice.* Vol. 1: *The American Experience.* New York: Academic Press.

Strasburger, Milton (1915). "A Plea for the Reform of the Interior Court." 22 *Cases and Comment* 20.

Stuart, Richard B., Leroy A. Lott, Jr. (1972). "Behavioral Contracting with Delinquents: A Cautionary Note." 3 *Journal of Behavioral Therapy and Experimental Psychiatry* 161.

Stuart, Richard B., Tony Tripodi, Sirinika Jayaratne, and Donald Camburn (1976). "An Experiment in Social Engineering in Serving the Families of Predelinquents." 4 *Journal of Abnormal Child Psychology* 243.

Stulberg, Joseph B. (1975). "A Civil Alternative to Criminal Prosecution." 39 *Albany Law Review* 359.

Sumner, Colin (1979). *Reading Ideologies: An Investigation into the Marxist Theory of Ideology and Law.* New York: Academic Press.

———— (1983). "Law, Legitimation and the Advanced Capitalist State: The Jurisprudence and Social Theory of Jurgen Habermas," in D. Sugarman, ed., *Legality, Ideology and the State.* London: Academic Press.

Susskind, Lawrence, and Connie Ozawa (1983). "Mediated Negotiation in the Public Sector: Mediator Accountability and the Public Interest Problem." 27 *American Behavioral Scientist* 255.

Taylor, Frederick W. (1911). *Scientific Management.* New York: Harper & Brothers.

The Mooter. (1977–1980). Pittsburgh: Grassroots Citizen Dispute Resolution Clearinghouse.

Therborn, Goran (1980). *The Ideology of Power and the Power of Ideology.* London: New Left Books.

Thompson, E. P. (1975). *Whigs and Hunters.* New York: Pantheon Books.

Tomasic, Roman (1982). "Mediation as an Alternative to Adjudication: Rhetoric and Reality in the Neighborhood Justice Movement," in R. Tomasic and M. Feeley, eds. *Neighborhood Justice: Assessment of an Emerging Idea*. New York: Longman.

Tomasic, Roman, and Malcolm M. Feeley eds. (1982). *Neighborhood Justice: Assessment of an Emerging Idea*. New York: Longman.

Trubek, David M. (1981). "Studying Courts in Context." 15 *Law & Society Review* 485.

Trubek, David M., Joel B. Grossman, William L. F. Felstiner, Herbert M. Kritzer, and Austin Sarat (1983a). *Civil Litigation Research Project Final Report*. Part A and B, Madison, WI: Dispute Processing Research Program.

Trubek, David M., Austin Sarat, William L. F. Felstiner, Herbert M. Kritzer, and Joel B. Grossman (1983b). "The Cost of Ordinary Litigation." 31 *UCLA Law Review* 72.

Turkel, Gerald (1980). "Legitimation, Authority, and Consensus Formation." 8 *International Journal of the Sociology of Law* 19.

Unger, Roberto Mangabeira (1976). *Law in Modern Society*. New York: Free Press.

United States House of Representatives Judiciary Committee (1977). "Hearings on the State of the Judiciary and Access to Justice." 95th Congress, 1st Session.

United States House of Representatives Judiciary Committee (1978). "Hearings Before the Subcommittee on Courts, Civil Liberties, and the Administration of Justice on S. 957, Dispute Resolution Act." 95th Congress, 2nd Session.

Van Alstyne, William (1968). "The Demise of the Right-Privilege Distinction." 81 *Harvard Law Review* 1439.

Vance, William (1917). "A Proposed Court of Conciliation." 1 *Minnesota Law Review* 105.

Vanderbilt, Arthur T. (1955). *The Challenge of Law Reform*. Princeton: University Press.

Vanlandingham, Kenneth E. (1964). "The Decline of the Justice of the Peace." 12 *University of Kansas Law Review* 389.

Vera Institute (1977). *Felony Arrests: Their Prosecution and Disposition in New York City's Courts*. New York: Vera Institute of Justice.

Verkuil, P. R. (1976). "A Study of Informal Adjudication Procedures." 43 *University of Chicago Law Review* 739.

Vidmar, Neil (1980). "Justice Motives and Other Psychological Factors in the Development and Resolution of Disputes," in M. J.

Lerner and S. C. Lerner, eds., *The Justice Motive in Social Behavior*. New York: Plenum Press.

Virtue, Maxine Boord (1953). "Improving the Structure of Courts." 187 *Annals of the American Academy of Political and Social Science* 141.

Volcansek, Mary (1977). "Conventional Wisdom of Court Reform," in L. Berkson, S. Hays, and S. Carbon, eds., *Managing the State Courts*. St. Paul, MN: West Publishing Co.

Vorenberg, E., and J. Vorenberg (1973). "Early Diversion from the Criminal Justice System: Practice in Search of a Theory," in L. E. Ohlin, ed. *Prisoners in America*. Englewood Cliffs, NJ: Prentice Hall.

Wahrhaftig, Paul (1977). "Lay Mediators—Are We Reinventing the Justice of the Peace?" in P. Wahrhaftig, ed., *The Citizen Dispute Resolution Organizer's Handbook*. Grassroots Citizen Dispute Resolution Clearinghouse, Philadelphia: American Friends Service Committee.

——— (1978). "Citizens Dispute Resolution: A Blue Chip Investment in Community Growth." 1978 *Pretrial Services Annual Journal*.

——— (1982). An Overview of Community-Oriented Citizen Dispute Resolution Programs in the United States," in R. Abel, ed., *The Politics of Informal Justice*. vol. 1: *The American Experience*. New York: Academic Press.

Walker, Samuel (1977). *A Critical History of Police Reform*. Lexington, MA: Lexington Books.

——— (1980). *Popular Justice: A History of American Criminal Justice*. New York: Oxford University Press.

Wechsler, Herbert (1959). "Toward Neutral Principles of Constitutional Law." 73 *Harvard Law Review* 1.

Weisbrod, Burton, Joel F. Handler, and Neil K. Komesar, eds., (1978). *Public Interest Law*. Berkeley: University of California Press.

Werner, Percy (1914). "Voluntary Tribunals: A Democratic Ideal." 2 *Virginia Law Review* 276.

——— (1919). "Voluntary Tribunals: A Democratic Ideal for the Adjudication of Private Differences Which Give Rise to Civil Actions." 3 *Journal of the American Judicature Society* 101.

Wickersham Commission (1974). "Petty Offenses and Interior Courts," in J. Robertson, ed., *Rough Justice: Perspectives in Lower Criminal Courts*. Cambridge, MA: Little, Brown (first published in 1931).

Wiebe, Robert H. (1967). *The Search for Order 1877–1920*. New York: Hill and Wang.

Wilkinson, J. Harvie (1976). "*Goss v. Lopez*: The Supreme Court as School Superintendent," in P. Kurland, ed., *The Supreme Court Review*. Chicago: University of Chicago Press.

Willoughby, W. F. (1929). *Principles of Judicial Administration*. Washington, D.C.: The Brookings Institution.

Wilson, James Q. (1968). *Varieties of Police Behavior*. Cambridge, MA: Harvard University Press.

Wolfe, Alan (1977). *The Limits of Legitimacy*. New York: Free Press.

Wright, Erik Olin (1978). *Class, Crisis and the State*. London: New Left Books.

Yale Law Journal (1974). "Comment: Pretrial Diversion from the Criminal Process." 83 *Yale Law Journal* 827.

————— (1979). "Dispute Resolution: Forward." 88 *Yale Law Journal* 905.

Yngvesson, Barbara (1985). "Legal Ideology and Community Justice in the Clerk's Office." 9 *Legal Studies Forum* 71.

Yngvesson, Barbara, and Patricia Hennessey (1975). "Small Claims Complex Disputes: A Review of the Small Claims Literature." 9 *Law & Society Review* 219.

Zemans, Frances Kahn (1983). "Legal Mobilization: The Neglected Role of the Law in the Political System." 77 *American Political Science Review* 690.

Zimring, Franklin E. (1974). "Measuring the Impact of Pretrial and Diversion from the Criminal Justice System." 41 *University of Chicago Law Review* 224.

Zunser, Charles (1926). "The Domestic Relations Courts." 125 *The Annals of the American Academy of Political and Social Science* 114.

COURT CASES

Bailey v. Richardson (341 U.S. 918, 1951).

Goldberg v. Kelley (397 U.S. 254, 1970).

Goss v. Lopez (419 U.S. 566, 1975).

In re Gault (387 U.S. 1, 1967).

Morrissey v. Brewer (408 U.S. 471, 1971).

Tummey v. Ohio (273 U.S. 510, 1927).

LEGISLATION

H.R. 2482 (1977). "Consumer Controversies Resolution Act." 95th Congress, 1st Session, January 26, 1977.

H.R. 2965 (1977). "Consumer Controversies Resolution Act." 95th Congress, 1st Session, February 2, 1977.

H.R. 2863 (1979). "Dispute Resolution Act." H.R. 96th Congress, 1st Session, March 13, 1979.

S. 957 (1978). "Dispute Resolution Act." H.R. 95th Congress, 2nd Session, July 27, August 2, 1978.

Index

Abel, Richard, 38 n.19, 132 n.9, 138, 163 n.4

Access to justice: 22-23, 49, 64, 75; and barriers to justice, 30-31, 98; congressional hearings on, 73, 76-77; for consumers, 96; and contemporary judicial management, 64; and due process in public institutions, 91. *See also* Judicial management; Judicial reform

Adjudication process: 16, 44, 51; and decentralized management of courts, 65, 67; limits of 137; limits of, 137; of racial disputes, 90; rationalization of, 44, 69-70 n.2, 169-70. *See also* Court capacity; Court management; Judicial management; Racial disputes

Administration of justice, 1, 9, 25, 48. *See also* Court reform; Judicial reform

Adversarial posture, 93

Adversarial process, 1, 12

Alienation, from lower courts, 30-31, 35

Alternative dispute resolution: 1-3, 34, 99, 140; community-based, 76, 86-87, 171-73; and cost saving, 75; court-based, 86-87, 100 n.3, 107, 171-73; ideology of, 34, 139, 171; incentives to participate in, 105; institutionalizing, 85, 131 n.1, 172; and legal education, 72 n.15; models, 86-87; professionalization of, 71 n.15, 172; as public policy, 73-74; specialization within, 100 n.6. *See also* Alternative dispute resolution program; Dispute resolution; Grass roots dispute resolution; Informal dispute processing

Alternative dispute resolution programs: 1, 131 n.5, 132 n.6; Brooklyn Dispute Resolution Center, 155, 163-64 n.5; Citizen Dispute Settlement Program (Orlando, Florida), 75,

About the Author

CHRISTINE B. HARRINGTON is an Assistant Professor in the Department of Politics at New York University. She has contributed to *Policy Implementation, The Politics of Informal Justice,* and *Law & Policy.*